A SCHOOL GRAMMAR
OF MODERN GERMAN

A SCHOOL GRAMMAR
OF MODERN GERMAN

BY

F. R. H. McLELLAN, M.A.

*Director of Modern Language Studies
at Mill Hill School*

CAMBRIDGE
AT THE UNIVERSITY PRESS
1928

CAMBRIDGE
UNIVERSITY PRESS

University Printing House, Cambridge CB2 8BS, United Kingdom

Cambridge University Press is part of the University of Cambridge.

It furthers the University's mission by disseminating knowledge in the pursuit of
education, learning and research at the highest international levels of excellence.

www.cambridge.org
Information on this title: www.cambridge.org/9781316612682

© Cambridge University Press 1928

First published 1928
First paperback edition 2016

A catalogue record for this publication is available from the British Library

ISBN 978-1-316-61268-2 Paperback

CONTENTS

PREFACE

In these days the study of German usually begins with a "Course" covering about a year's work, after which a systematic treatment of the grammar is necessary. It is for pupils at this stage that the present work is primarily designed.

It has been the author's endeavour to limit the scope of the book to the requirements of the first three or four years, while omitting nothing that a pupil can reasonably be expected to learn during that period.

As the book is intended for school use, explanations are brief: it is for the master to supplement them. At the same time it is hoped that there is enough explanatory matter to guide a student using it for independent work.

The syntax of each part of speech is dealt with immediately after its accidence, and a large number of cross-references are provided.

I am indebted to my old friend and former colleague, Mr E. W. Hallifax, for much valuable assistance.

F. R. H. M.

1928

INTRODUCTION

The German Language.

Both English and German belong to the Aryan or Indo-European family of languages, whose most ancient literary monuments are the Sanskrit Vedas, a collection of religious poems, preserved by oral tradition and dating from about the 15th century B.C. From these, and from other members of the family, we can obtain a fairly clear idea of the parent language.

The chief branches of the Aryan family of languages, arranged according to geographical distribution, are :

	Germanic	Lithuanian			
Celtic		Slavonic			
	Latin	Greek	Armenian	Persian	Sanskrit.

The Germanic branch is characterised by a change or shifting of the consonants, which appears to have taken place during the three centuries preceding the Christian era. This process was first successfully investigated by the Brothers Grimm (famous not only as grammarians but as the compilers of Grimms Märchen), who called it the Erste or Germanische Lautverschiebung. The general principles governing this and the subsequent change (Zweite or Hochdeutsche Lautverschiebung) are known as Grimm's Law.

Aryan	*Germanic*
Tenues (Unvoiced Stops) become	Spirants (Fricatives)
P, T, K	F, TH, CH or H
Aspirates become	Mediae (Voiced Stops)
BH, DH, GH	B, D, G
Mediae (Voiced Stops) become	Tenues (Unvoiced Stops)
B, D, G	P, T, K.

These changes may be illustrated by examples from Latin

and English, in which the Aryan and Germanic consonants, respectively, have been preserved, though it will be noticed that Latin has lost the aspirates and replaces BH and DH by F, and GH by H; while English replaces the lost fricative CH by H, Y or W.

Lat.	Pater	Ten-uis	Corn-u
Eng.	Father	THin	Horn
Lat.	Fer-o (= bher-o)	For-is (= dhor-is)	Hort-us
Eng.	Bear	Door	Garden
Lat.	turB-a	eDo	juG-um
Eng.	thorP	eaT	yoKe.

There are two main exceptions to this rule:

(*a*) P, T, K following S, are not changed; thus *sp*ec-ere, *sp*y; *sc*utula (scutella), *sc*uttle; *st*a-re, *st*and;

(*b*) P, T, K in many cases become B, D, G instead of the corresponding spirants. These cases were accounted for by Verner (1877) by a change of stress accent from the parent language. Thus Aryan paTér, Old Eng. fáDer; *father*.

THE GERMANIC LANGUAGES are :

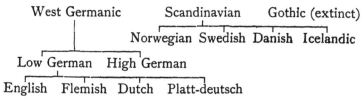

The language now known as German is that which appears on the table as High German, and was separated from the Low German languages by a second shifting of the consonants, Zweite or Hochdeutsche Lautverschiebung, which took place between the 6th and 8th centuries after Christ, and affected the dialects spoken in Southern and Central Germany, the change being more marked as we go southward and reaching its maximum in Switzerland. From the time of Charlemagne these dialects were known as *diutisk* or *deutsch*, i.e. the language of the people.

The Germanic	P, T, K	now became	F, S (TS, Z), CH.
„	F, TH, CH	„	B, D, G.
„	B, D, G	„	P, T, K.

This second change was not so far-reaching as the first, and the Germanic B and G seem to have been almost entirely unaffected, though they have been placed in the above table for the sake of symmetry. It should be realised however that B, D, G are in many cases pronounced P, T, K, especially in Central and Southern Germany.

A list of Cognates will make the kinship of Latin, English and German more evident.

Lat. T.	Tres	Turba	Tonitr-us	Torr-eo	Ten-uis	Teg-o
Eng. TH.	THree	THorp	THunder	THirst	THin	THatch
Ger. D.	Drei	Dorf	Donner	Durst	Dünn	Dach

Lat. P.	raPio	sePtem	suPer
Eng. F, V.	reaVe	seVen	oVer
Ger. B.	rauB	sieBen	üBer

Lat. K.	deC(em)	oC-ulus	seC-o
Eng. H. (gh, ow, y)	(twen)tY	eYe	sAW
Ger. G.	(zwan)ziG	auGe	säG-en

Lat. F.	Fer-o	Frater	Fag-us	Fod-io	Frang-o
Eng. B.	Bear	Brother	Beech	Bed	Break
Ger. (P) B.	ge-Bär-en	Bruder	Buch-e	Bett, Beet	Brech-en

Lat. (TH) F.	Fer-us	For-es	Fing-o	Fung-or
Eng. D.	Deer	Door	Dough	Dough-ty
Ger. T.	Tier	Tür	Teig	Taug-en

Lat.	H.	Haed-us	Host-is	Hort-us			
Eng.	G.	Goat	Guest	Gard-en			
Ger.	(K) G.	Geiss	Gast	Gart-en			

Lat.	B.	turB-a	laB-o		luBric-us		
Eng.	P.	thorP	sleeP		sliPPery		
Ger.	F.	dorF	schlaF-en, schlaFF		schlüPFrig		

Lat.	D.	eD-o	Duo	quiD	viDi	peD-em	Decem
Eng.	T.	eaT	Two	whaT	wiT	fooT	Ten
Ger.	S, TS.	eSS-en	zwei	waS	weiSS	fuSS	zehn

Lat.	G.	franG-o	juG-um	viG-ilo	eGo	
Eng.	K.	breaK	yoKe	waKe	L. G. iK	
Ger.	CH.	breCH-en	joCH	waCHen	iCH.	

THE VOCABULARY of the German language contains a large number of words borrowed from other languages, though it is in this respect much purer than English.

From contact with the neighbouring tribes, a few *Celtic words* found their way into the language, including Amt, *office*, Düne, *dune*, Falke, *falcon*, Reich, *kingdom*, welsch, *foreign*.

From the ROMANS, who planted colonies on German soil (e.g. Cologne, Köln = *colonia*; Strassburg, the fortress on the road), came terms relating to *architecture*, such as Fenster, *fenestra*, Kammer, *camera*, Keller, *cellarium*, Mauer, *murus*, Pforte, *porta*, Turm, *turris*.

Military terms:
Kaiser, Strasse.

Domestic terms:

Tisch	*discus*	Tafel	*tabula*	Schüssel	*scutula*
Spiegel	*specula*	Sack	*saccus*	Korb	*corbis*
Kiste	*cista*	Leinen	*linum*	Butter	*butyrum*
Käse	*caseus.*				

Many *plants and fruits* introduced by the Romans still bear
their Latin names:

Pfeffer	*piper*	Senf	*sinapi*	Minze	*mentha*
Kohl	*caulis*	Rettich	*radix*	Wein	*vinum*
Kirsche	*cerasus*	Pflaume	*prunum*	Birne	*pirum*
Rose	*rosa*	Lilie	*lilium*	Veilchen	*viola.*

Religious terms introduced by the early missionaries
include:

Kloster	*claustrum*	Priester	*presbyter*	Mönch	*monachus*
Münster	*monasterium*	Abt	*abbas*	Kreuz	*crux*
Kirche	*cyriace*	Pfarre	*parochia*	Teufel	*diabolus.*

In the 12th century FRANCE was the centre of chivalry, and
added to the vocabularies of its neighbours a number of words
dealing with *the court and the field.* Such are:

Posaune	*buisine*	Flöte	*flûte*	Tanz	*danse*
Turnier	*tournoi*	Lanze	*lance*	Harnisch	*harnais*
Abenteuer	*aventure*	Sold	*solde*	Koppel	*couple*

(leash of hounds).

Some words originally German were re-imported in French
guise, e.g. Herold, O.F. *héralt*; Banner, *bannière.*

With the Renaissance a flood of LATIN and GREEK words
swept over Europe, and German did not escape. In 1572 a
grammarian was able to count no fewer than 2000 Latin
words in common use. These were, mainly,

Terms relating to Study:

Aula	*college hall*	Katheder	*lecturer's desk*	Podium	*dais*
Glossar	*glossary*	Karzer	*cells*	Examen	*examination*

Botanik, Geographie, Geometrie, addieren, subtrahieren, etc.

Medical terms:

Abszess, Indisposition, Katarrh.

Legal terms:

Klient, Magistrat, Prozess, Advokat, Majorität.

Political terms:

Kommissar, Regent, Monarch, Majestät (first used by Charles V).

Even *Proper Names* were latinised. Schneider was changed to Sartor, Weber to Textor, Schmied to Faber. Peters became Petri, Jacobs Jacobi. Melanchthon is a Greek rendering of Schwarzerd.

The predominance of FRANCE in the 17th century has left its mark on the German language. Germans with any pretention to elegance loaded their speech with French words, such as:

elegant, brillant, charmant, galant, honett, nett, nobel, Kabale, Intrige, Schikane,

all of which are still current. Even the family circle was invaded by Onkel and Tante, Cousin and Cousine, while Grossvater and Grossmutter are translated from *grand-père* and *grand'mère.*

Many *military terms* were adopted from the French, including: Armee, Parade, Bataillon, Brigade, General, Artillerie, Infanterie

ITALIAN has contributed *musical terms*, e.g. Sopran, Alt, Bass, Piano, etc., and many commercial terms, e.g. franko, netto, bankrott, Conto.

ENGLISH has given words connected with *sport*, e.g. Handikap, Steeplechase, Sport, boxen, starten, Dogge, Tennis; and *political terms*, e.g. Bill, Strike, Meeting.

Although non-German terms are being constantly introduced for new inventions, e.g. Auto, Aeroplan, Radio, Kinematograph, there is a healthy tendency, which should be observed by all who write German, never to use a foreign term when there is a convenient native word to express the same idea.

I. THE SOUNDS AND CHARACTERS OF GERMAN

1.   PHONETIC SYSTEM.

A detailed account of the phonetics of German is beyond the scope of this book. The table below is a simple arrangement of the sounds of the German language, expressed in the symbols of the Association Phonétique Internationale. For practice in pronunciation examples will be found in § 5.

Table of Sounds

		Laryngeal	Velar	Palatal	Lingual (Dental)	Labial
Consonants	Plosive	ʔ	k ɡ		t d	p b
	Nasal		ŋ		n	m
	Lateral				l	
	Trilled				r	
	Spirant	h	x	ç j	ʃ s z	f v
Vowels	Closed		u	y i		
	Half-closed		o ə	ø e		
	Half-open		ɔ	œ ɛ		
	Open		ɑ			

Note. There are many varieties of *R*. That shown above, formed by trilling the tip of the tongue, is the sound generally used on the stage, and is perhaps the easiest for an Englishman to acquire. The *R* most commonly heard in conversation is formed by trilling the uvula, and closely resembles the velar spirant x.

2.   THE GERMAN ALPHABET.

Name of letter (A.P.I.)	German characters		Script		Latin characters
ɑː	𝔄	a			a
beː	𝔅	b			b
tseː	ℭ	c			c
deː	𝔇	b			d
eː	𝔈	e			e
ɛf	𝔉	f			f
geː	𝔊	g			g
haː	𝔥	h			h
iː	ℑ	i			i
jɔt	ℑ	j			j
kaː	𝔎	k			k
ɛl	𝔏	l			l
ɛm	𝔐	m			m
ɛn	𝔑	n			n
oː	𝔇	o			o
peː	𝔓	p			p
kuː	𝔔	q			q
ɛr	𝔑	r			r
ɛs	𝔖	ſ, s			s
teː	𝔗	t			t
uː	𝔘	u			u

Name of letter (A.P.I.)	German characters		Script		Latin characters
fau	𝔙	𝔳			v
ve:	𝔚	𝔴			w
Iks	𝔛	ᶲ			x
i'psi·lon	𝔜	𝔶			y
tset	ℨ	ᵹ			z

3. SPECIMEN OF GERMAN SCRIPT.

Es war einmal ein Müller.
Der war arm, aber er hatte
eine schöne Tochter. Nun
traf es sich, daß er mit dem
König zu sprechen kam, und
um sich ein Ansehen zu geben,
sagte er zu ihm: „Ich habe
eine Tochter, die kann Stroh
zu Gold spinnen."
London, den 27. IX. 1928.

4.   Notes.

(a) **Umlaut.** The vowels a, o, u, are subject to modification
or Umlaut. They are then written ä, ö, ü, and pronounced
ε, ø or œ, y, respectively.

The symbol ˮ represents the letter e, and is not to be confused with the diæresis.

The capitals of modified vowels are generally printed Ä́, Ö́, Ǘ;
but sometimes Ä́, Ö́, Ǘ, or Ae, Oe, Ue.

(b) **Diphthongs.** The diphthongs ai, au, ei, eu, are pronounced aⁱ, aᵘ, aⁱ, ɔø respectively; au modifies to äu, pronounced ɔø.

(c) **S.** ß (runbes S) is used at the end of a word, or of one
component of a compound; in all other cases ſ (langes S):
das Gras, Grashalm, des Grases, sie sehen.

(d) **SS.** ſſ (langes Doppel-S) is used only when preceded
by a short vowel and followed by another vowel, as in laſſen,
Schloſſes, Nüſſe; in all other cases ß (runbes Doppel-S): ließen,
läßt, Nuß, Schloß, beßrer (=beſſerer).

The second *s* is not to be thought of as a *z*. When using
Latin script, write either *ss* or ß. *sz* appears only in compounds, such as *ausziehen,* ausziehen, where the *s* and *z* are in
different syllables.

5. Examples for Illustration and Practice of the
                      German Sounds.

a *long*	aː	Bahn, Abend, baben, haben, Glas, Haar.
a *short*	a	alt, haſt, ganz, Stabt, scharf, Arm.
ä *long*	εː	spät, täglich, Bäder, Jäger, Gläſer.
ä *short*	ε	hätte, älter, gänzlich, Städte, Schärfe, ärmlich.
ai	aⁱ	Mai, Kaiſer, Laib, Mainz, Saite.
au	aᵘ	Haus, laut, bauen, Raub, aus.
äu	ɔø	Häuſer, läuten, Gebäube, Räuber, äußerſt.

b (*final = p*)	b	Bäcker, Gebäck, Brot; bergab, abgehen, lobst.
ch	x	Bach, Buch, rauchen, doch, hoch.
ch	ç	Bäche, Bücher, mich, euch, reich, Kelch, Mädchen.
ch *in Greek words*		Charakter, Chor; Chemie (kar'aktər, ko:r, çemi).
d	d	Dach, Dorf, drei, ander, Bruder.
d *final*	t	Bad, Jagd, Hund, Magd, sehend.
e *long*	e:	See, sehen, Reh, Ehre, werden, wert.
e *short*	ɛ	fett, Heft, besser, Herr, gesperrt.
e *unstressed*	ə	Bäder, baden, Gebirge, gesagt, Stiefel.
ei	aⁱ	Leiter, Teil, fein, steil, heiter.
eu	ɔᵛ	neu, Eule, Freude, Heu, streuen.
g *initial* or *medial*		
	g	ganz, gleich, Gebirge, Berge, sage, borge.
g *final*	k, x, ç	Tag, häufig, gebirgig, Berg, sagst, borgst.
h *initial*	h	haben, Herbst, heute, Hund.
h *mute*		sehen, gehen, ziehen, mähen, Naht.
i *long*	i:	wider, Mine, Tiger, ihnen, irisch.
i *short*	ɪ	Widder, Minister, nicht, sitzen, mit.
ie	i:	Lied, siehst, Offizier, Geographie.
ie	jə	Familie (fami·ljə), Asien (a:zjən), Spanier (spa·njər).
j	j	Jahr, jährlich, Jubiläum, Juli, Jäger.
ng	ŋ	singen, Sänger, lang, länger, Bingen.
o *long*	o:	groß, hoch, Monat, Mond, Boot, Mohre.
ö *long*	ø:	größer, höher, böse, hören, gehört, zerstört.
o *short*	ɔ	Schloß, Loch, Kopf, Sonne, Wolle.
ö *short*	œ	Schlösser, Löcher, Köpfe, zwölf, Mörder.
qu	kv	Quelle, quer, quitt, Quecksilber, Quacksalber.
r	r	Ehre, Ähre, Ohr, Arm, Schirm.
s *final*	s	Glas, Gras, Haus, Fels, Ochs, Gans.
s *medial*, after consonants other than *l, m, n, r*		
	s	Ochsen, Lotse, obsolet, Erbsen.
s *initial*	z	Sohn, Sonne, sitzen, sagen, sehen, singen.
s *medial*, after vowels or *l, m, n, r*		
	z	Gläser, Gräser, Häuser, Amsel, Gänse, Börse.

ſch	ſ	Schein, Schloß, raſch; but Häus=chen.
ſp, ſt *initial*	ſp, ſt	Sprung, ſprechen, Stabt, Straße.
tion	tsjoːn	Nation, Revolution, Senſation.
u *long*	uː	Kuh, Fuß, Gruß, tun.
u *short*	u	Mutter, Schuß, Suppe, unter.
ü *long*	yː	Kühe, Füße, grüßen, über, Bücher.
ü *short*	y	Mütter, Schüſſe, Sünde, hüpfen.
v	f	von, vier, verzeihen, Veilchen, Vogt, aktiv.
w	v	wer, was, Wall, ſchwingen, Zwerg, ſchwören.
y	y, i, ɪ	Gymnaſium, Hypothek, Pſycholog, Zyklus.
z	ts	Zwei, Kreuz, zerbrechen, ächzen, Zahn, Zug.

f, k, l, m, n, p, t, χ are pronounced approximately as in English.

Foreign words are usually pronounced as in the language of origin.

Stress Accent (Betonung).

6. The accent falls on the root syllable, i.e. the first, except where there is a prefix:

fließen, to flow; flüſſig, liquid; Flüſſigkeit, a liquid; Flüſſigkeiten, liquids.

7. The chief exceptions are:

lebéndig, living; Forélle, trout; Holúnder, elder-tree; Wachólber, juniper-tree; Lawíne, avalanche; ſchmarótzen, to sponge; krakeélen, to brawl; Horníſſe, hornet; Hermelín, ermine; luthériſch, Lutheran.

For the accentuation of words with prefixes, see §§ 522 sqq.

8. In compounds the accent falls on the determinative word, i.e. the one that limits the other. These present no difficulty, the English rule being the same:

Sónnenſchein, sunshine; Rótkehlchen, redbreast; zweibeinig, two-legged.

9. Note that these words have a second and lighter accent, which it is especially important to observe in long compounds:

Sónnen-aùfgang, sunrise; Vólks-schùle, elementary school.

Compare the accent in Vólks-schul-lèhrer, elementary school-master; Vólks-schul-lehrer-seminàr, training-college for elementary schoolmasters; Léhrer-seminàr, training-college.

10. Foreign words are usually accented on the last syllable (not counting any German suffix):

Philosóph, philosóphisch, Telephón, telephónisch, kolossál, Majestát, Román.

Some, however, keep the Latin accent on the penultimate:

Dóktor, Pástor, Proféssor, Kónsul (*pl.* Doktóren, etc.).

Modern loan-words are accented as in the original language:

Tornádo, Signóra, Novélle, Etiquétte, Ballón, Hándikap.

11. THE GLOTTAL STOP (der Kehlkopfverschluß).

A stressed syllable beginning with a vowel is preceded by a rapid closing of the glottis, the position of the vocal chords being as if the speaker were about to cough. The result is a very strong expulsion of breath at the beginning of the syllable; this is one of the most marked features of German pronunciation. Distinguish between vereist, fər'aist, 'frozen over,' and verreist, fər'raist, 'travelling.'

12. DIVISION INTO SYLLABLES (die Silbentrennung).

Each syllable begins, where possible, with a consonant:

ge-ben, Re-vol-ver, ge-bro-chen, grö-ßer.

Certain groups of consonants are indivisible: ch, sch, ß, st, ph (= f), th (= t):

ge-stan-den, Ma-schi-ne, Te-le-phon, A-the-ist.

Other groups are divided between two syllables:

Pin-sel, Hun-ger, Sil-ber, Damp-fer, Künst-ler.

Compounds are divided into their component parts:

hier=in, dar=aus, Erz=engel, aus=üben.

In dividing a word at the end of a line, avoid leaving a single letter; thus Ameise must be divided, not A=meise, but Amei=se or not at all; ausüben should be divided aus=üben, not ausü=ben.

Note that ck when divided becomes kk: Bäk=ker.

CAPITAL LETTERS (große Anfangsbuchstaben).

13. German uses capitals more freely than English, especially in

(*a*) All Nouns: das Buch, die Bücher.

(*b*) Words used as Nouns: das Für und Wider, the pros and cons; das Edle, the noble, nobility.

(*c*) Adjectives following etwas, manches, nichts, alles, viel:

nichts Merkwürdiges, nothing remarkable;
etwas Schönes, something beautiful.

(*d*) Sie, Er, Ihr, when used for the 2nd person; likewise all their cases, and their possessive adjectives and pronouns:

Wie geht's Ihnen? How do you do?
Wie heißt Ihr Freund? What is your friend's name?
Lasse Er mich in Ruhe! Leave me in peace.

(*e*) Du and Dein, in letters:

Herzliche Grüße an Deine Eltern! Kind regards to your parents.
Warum hast Du nicht geschrieben? Why did you not write?

14. N.B. Adjectives formed from proper names *do not take a capital*, except those in =isch, ='sch, from names of persons, and those in =er from place-names:

die britische Flotte, the British fleet; die Müller'sche Familie (die Familie Müller), the Müller family; das Münchener Bier, Munich beer.

15.   PUNCTUATION (die Interpunktion).

Note the following divergences from English usage:

(*a*) *Every* subordinate clause is separated by a comma from its governing clause:

> Das Buch, das Sie lesen, taugt nichts.
> The book you are reading is worthless.

(*b*) Co-ordinate clauses joined by a conjunction are separated by a comma when there is a change of subject, not otherwise:

> Er ging nach Amerika und starb in Neu-York.
> He went to America and died in New York.

(*c*) Exclamation-marks are used after all commands and exclamations:

> Bitte, bleiben Sie sitzen!—Danke!
> Please don't stand up.—Thank you.

Note the position of the inverted commas.

> „Halt!" rief er. "Stop!" he cried.

II. DEFINITE & INDEFINITE ARTICLES

(der bestimmte Artikel, der unbestimmte Artikel)

DECLENSION.

16. (i) Definite Article.

	Masc.	Fem.	Neut.	Plural *All Genders*
Nom.	der	die	das	die
Acc.	den	die	das	die
Gen.	des	der	des	der
Dat.	dem	der	dem	den.

The following contractions of Preposition + Article are permissible, when the article is unemphatic:

(*a*) Dem (masc. or neut.) after bei, von, zu,
forming beim, vom, zum;

(*b*) Das after auf, durch, für, um,
forming aufs, durchs, fürs, ums;

(*c*) Dem or Das after an, hinter, in, über, unter, vor,
forming am, hinterm, im, überm, unterm, vorm;
ans, hinters, ins, übers, unters, vors.

(*d*) Der (dat. sing. fem.) after zu, forming zur.
Note um's Himmels willen, for Heaven's sake; where um's = um des.

17. (ii) Indefinite Article.

	Masc.	Fem.	Neut.	
Nom.	ein	eine	ein	*No*
Acc.	einen	eine	ein	*Plural*
Gen.	eines	einer	eines	
Dat.	einem	einer	einem.	

USE OF THE ARTICLES.

The Definite Article is used

18. (1) As a weakened demonstrative, its commonest use:

Das Haus gefällt mir nicht.   I don't like the house.

19. (2) With nouns used in a general sense:

Die Bauern führen ein gesundes Leben.   Peasants lead a healthy life.

Also in the singular:

Der Bauer führt ein gesundes Leben.

20. N.B. (*a*) Abstract nouns and names of substances, when thus used, take the Article:

Die Tugend belohnt sich selbst.   Virtue is its own reward.

Das Brot ist teuer dieses Jahr.   Bread is dear this year.

21. (*b*) But names of substances used partitively stand without the Article:

Geben Sie mir Brot, Butter und Schweizerkäse!

Give me some bread and butter and Gruyère cheese.

22. (*c*) As in French, the Article before abstract nouns, etc., is often omitted in proverbs:

Armut ist keine Schande.   Poverty is not a disgrace.

23. (3) Distributively:

Wir fuhren 70 Km. die Stunde.

We were travelling at 70 km. an hour.

Diese Postkarten kosten 20 Pfennig das Stück.

These post-cards cost 20 pfennigs apiece.

24. (4) With proper nouns:

(*a*) Frequently with names of persons, to show the case; but it should not be used thus except where absolutely necessary:

Ich habe dem Herrn Schulze Onkel Paul vorgestellt.

I have introduced Uncle Paul to Herr Schulze.

25. (*b*) With most geographical and topographical names:

der Rhein, the Rhine   der Bodensee, Lake Constance
der Vesuv, Vesuvius   der Elsaß, Alsace
die Schweiz, Switzerland   die Hochstraße, High Street
die Türkei, Turkey   die Tschecho-slowakei, Czechoslovakia
die Vereinigten Staaten, the United States.

But not with names of towns or islands, or neuter names of countries and continents:

Helgoland, Heligoland; Frankreich, France; Italien, Italy; Tirol, the Tyrol; Genf, Geneva; Australien, Australia.

N.B. der Himmel, Heaven; die Hölle, Hell; das Paradies, Paradise.

26. (*c*) Regularly when an adjective precedes, and sometimes before a title:

der alte Fritz, Old Fritz (Friedrich der Grosse).
die Geschichte vom fliegenden Robert,
The Tale of Flying Robert (in *Struwwelpeter*).
das reiche Amerika, wealthy America.
Kaiser Franz, or der Kaiser Franz, the Emperor Francis.

N.B. Jung Siegfried, Alt-England, Alt-Heidelberg, Kleinasien, Großbritannien.

27. (5) With names of seasons, months, days, and in many other cases where it is idiomatically omitted in English:

im Herbst	in autumn
im August	in August
beim Frühstück	at breakfast
im Gefängnis	in prison
in der Kirche	at church
in der Schule	at school
zur See, auf der See	at sea
mit der Bahn	by train

mit der Post	by post
im Bette liegen	to be in bed
sich ins Bett legen	to go to bed
(but zu Bett gehen)	
die Nacht brach ein	night was falling.

28. (6) With parts of the body, clothing, etc., instead of the possessive adjective:

Er setzte den Hut auf. He put his hat on.

Frequently in conjunction with the dative of the personal pronoun:

Er hat mir auf den Fuß getreten. He has trod on my foot.

Ich habe mir den Fuß verrenkt. I have sprained my ankle.

29. (7) With zu after verbs of appointing, electing, etc.:

Der König von Preußen wurde zum deutschen Kaiser gewählt.
The King of Prussia was elected German Emperor.

Mache dich nicht zum Narren! Don't make a fool of yourself.

30. The **Definite Article** is omitted in many idiomatic phrases, such as:

bei einbrechender Nacht	at nightfall
von ganzem Herzen	with all my heart
Wort halten	to keep one's word.

And particularly with nouns used in pairs, e.g.

Mann und Maus, every living soul; Mann und Roß, horse and rider; Feuer und Schwert, fire and sword; Blut und Eisen, blood and iron.

31. The **Indefinite Article** is used almost as in English. Note its omission

(1) before a noun serving as complement to sein, werden, bleiben, especially when denoting rank, profession, nation:

Er ist Präfekt geworden. He has been made a prefect.

Ich bin und bleibe Soldat. I am a soldier, and will always be one.

32. (2) in many idiomatic expressions, e.g.

Das ist Schade	That is a pity
Angst haben	to be afraid
Hunger (Durst) haben	to be hungry (thirsty)
Recht (unrecht) haben	to be right (wrong)
Lust haben	to feel inclined
Kopfweh (Zahnweh) haben	to have a headache (toothache).

III. NOUNS

(das Hauptwort oder Substantiv)

GENDER OF NOUNS (das Geschlecht).

33. Gender is a grammatical term, and does not always correspond with sex. A few of the rules for determining gender are given here, but the golden rule is to learn every noun, as soon as met, with its definite article.

The first clue to the gender of a noun is its meaning; if that fails, the form usually helps.

34. **Masculine by Meaning** are

(*a*) Names of male beings:

der Mann, the man; der Löwe, the lion; der Satyr, the satyr.

But die Schildwache, sentry; die Person, person; das Mitglied, member; die Waise, orphan.

(*b*) Names of seasons, months, days:

der Herbst, autumn; der März, March; der Montag, Monday.

(*c*) Names of stones:

der Granit, granite; der Diamant, diamond.

35. **Masculine by Form** are

(*a*) Nouns ending in =ig, =ich, =ing, =ling:

der Honig, honey; der Teppich, carpet.

(*b*) Verb-stems without suffix, with or without Ablaut:

der Wurf (werfen), throw; der Fall (fallen), fall, case.

36. **Feminine by Meaning** are

(*a*) Names of female beings:

die Schwester, sister; die Göttin, goddess.

But das Weib, woman.

(*b*) Names of German rivers:

die Donau, Danube; die Oder, die Elbe.

But der Rhein, der Main, der Neckar.

37. Feminine by Form are

(*a*) Nouns in ‑ei, ‑heit, ‑keit, ‑schaft, ‑ung:

die Druckerei, printing; die Weisheit, wisdom; die Tapferkeit, bravery; die Gesellschaft, company; die Rechnung, account.

(*b*) Nouns in ‑e, not being the names of living beings:

die Blume, flower; die Länge, length.

But see § 39 (*c*).

(*c*) Those formed from verbs and ending in ‑d or ‑t:

die Schlacht (schlagen), battle; die Schuld (sollen), debt.

(*d*) Foreign nouns in ‑ie, ‑ion, ‑ik, ‑tät:

die Chemie, chemistry; die Auktion, auction; die Physik, physics; die Majestät, majesty.

38. Neuter by Meaning are

(*a*) Names of countries and continents:

Preußen, Prussia; Amerika, America.

But die Schweiz, Switzerland; die Türkei, Turkey; die Tschechoslowakei, Czechoslovakia; der Elsaß, Alsace.

(*b*) Names of metals:

das Gold, gold; das Eisen, iron.

But der Stahl, steel.

(*c*) Other parts of speech used as nouns:

das Fliegen, flying; das Für und Wider, the pros and cons; and such terms as das X, the letter X.

(But names of arithmetical figures are *feminine*: die Vier, the 4.)

39. Neuter by Form are

(*a*) Diminutives in ‑chen and ‑lein:

das Bißchen, the little bit; das Kindlein, the little child.

(*b*) Most nouns in -ſal, -ſel, -tum, and concrete nouns in -nis:

    das Schickſal, fate; das Scheuſal, monster;

        but die Mühſal, trouble; die Trübſal, affliction.

    das Altertum, antiquity;

        but der Reichtum, wealth; der Irrtum, error.

    das Gefängnis, prison; das Bildnis, portrait;

        but die Erlaubnis, permission.

(*c*) Most nouns derived from verbs, with prefix Ge-:

    das Geſchäft, business; das Geſchenk, present.

Often with final -e: das Gebäude, building; das Getöſe, din.

But der Gebrauch, use; der Gedanke, thought; der Geruch, smell;
der Geſang, song; der Geſchmack, taste; der Gewinn, gain;
die Geburt, birth; die Geduld, patience; die Gefahr, danger;
die Geſchichte, story; die Geſtalt, figure; die Gewalt, power.

40. Compound Nouns take the gender of the last component:

    der Blumenkohl, cauliflower; die Steinkohle, coal.

    der Winkelmeſſer, protractor; das Taſchenmeſſer, pocket-knife.

But das Wort, word; die Antwort, answer. Der Mut, mood; die Anmut, gracefulness; die Demut, humility; die Großmut, magnanimity. Der Teil, part; das Gegenteil, opposite; das Mittel, means; das Drittel, Viertel, uſw., third part, quarter, etc.

41. Note the following pairs:

der Erbe	heir	das Erbe	inheritance
der Band	volume	das Band	bond, fetter
der Bauer	peasant	das Bauer	bower, cage
der Chor	choir, chorus	das Chor	chancel
der Heide	heathen	die Heide	heath
der Hut	hat	die Hut	guard

der Kiefer	jaw	die Kiefer	fir-tree
der Kunde	customer	die Kunde	news
der Leiter	director	die Leiter	ladder
der Schild	shield	das Schild	sign-board
der See	lake	die See	sea
der Tor	fool	das Tor	gate
der Stift	pin	das Stift	foundation
die Mark	mark, money	das Mark	marrow
die Steuer	tax	das Steuer	rudder.

42. Feminine nouns are formed from masculines by adding -in:

> der Amerikaner, American; die Amerikanerin.

Umlaut takes place in monosyllables:

> der Storch, stork; die Störchin;

and in the one polysyllable

> der Franzose, Frenchman; die Französin.

43. Note:

der Prinz	prince	die Prinzessin
der Vater	father	die Mutter
der Sohn	son	die Tochter
der Bruder	brother	die Schwester
der Onkel	uncle	die Tante
der Neffe	nephew	die Nichte
der Bräutigam	bridegroom	die Braut
der Junggesell	bachelor	die Jungfer
der Kater	tom-cat	die Katze
der Herr	master	die Herrin
der Herr	gentleman	die Dame
der Herr	Mr	die Frau or das Fräulein.

DECLENSION OF NOUNS (Deflination ber Hauptwörter).

(An alternative treatment of §§ 44 to 59 is given in the Appendix.)

44. There are four Declensions—three strong and one weak.

The characteristic cases are the Genitive Singular and the Nominative Plural. When these are known, the others follow.

45. **All Feminine Nouns** are invariable in the singular. They are therefore unaffected by the rules of declension, except as regards their plural.

All Strong Nouns form the Gen. Sing. by adding ⸗es or ⸗s to the Nom.

All Weak Nouns add ⸗en or ⸗n throughout.

46. **In all Nouns** the Acc. and Gen. Plural are the same as the Nom. Pl.

In all Nouns the Dat. Pl. ends in ⸗n.

In all Strong Nouns, except those in § 51 (*a*), the Acc. Sing. is the same as the Nom. Sing.

47. **Umlaut in Nouns.** In many strong nouns the radical vowel is modified in the plural, a, o, u, au becoming ä, ö, ü, äu respectively. Saal has plural Säle.

No hard and fast rules can be laid down to show which nouns take the Umlaut; but note that modification takes place in

      All plurals in ⸗er;   **All fem. plurals in** ⸗e;
      No plurals in ⸗n;   **No neut. plurals in** ⸗e.

48. **Compound Nouns** are declined as the last component:

      Eingang, entrance, Eingänge;
      Weinglas, wine-glass, Weingläser.

But most compounds in ⸗mann take ⸗leute:

      Seemann, seaman, Seeleute;
      Hauptmann, captain, Hauptleute.

Staatsmann, statesman, and Ehemann, husband, have Staatsmänner, Ehemänner. Eheleute means married *people*.

49. SCHEME OF THE DECLENSIONS

	Characteristics		Umlaut	Nouns Included
	Gen. S.	*Nom. Pl.*		
I	ß	—	only in 26 nouns	(a) Masc. and neuters in ⸗el, ⸗en, ⸗er, ⸗chen, ⸗lein. (b) Neut. with prefix Ge⸗ and suffix ⸗e. (c) Mutter, Tochter (*with Umlaut*). (d) Käse.
II	eß or ß	e	usually	(a) The bulk of masculines. (b) All nouns in ⸗niß, ⸗sal. (c) Some 40 neut. monosyllabics (*no Umlaut*). (d) Some 35 fem. monosyllabics (*Umlaut*).
III	eß or ß	er	always	(a) Some 60 neuter monosyllabics. (b) 7 Compounds of Ge⸗. (c) 7 masculine monosyllabics. (d) Nouns in ⸗mal, ⸗tum.
IV	en or n	en or n	never	(a) Masculines in ⸗e. (b) 19 masculine monosyllabics. (c) 31 feminine monosyllabics. (d) Feminine polysyllabics, except those in I (c) and II (b). (e) Some foreign nouns (see §§ 66 sqq.).

50.   FIRST DECLENSION.

		summer	brother	young lady
Sing.	N.	der Sommer	der Bruder	das Fräulein
	A.	den Sommer	den Bruder	das Fräulein
	G.	des Sommer=s	des Bruder=s	des Fräulein=s
	D.	dem Sommer	dem Bruder	dem Fräulein
Plur.	N.	die Sommer	die Brüder	die Fräulein
	A.	die Sommer	die Brüder	die Fräulein
	G.	der Sommer	der Brüder	der Fräulein
	D.	den Sommer=n	den Brüder=n	den Fräulein.

Note that First-Declension nouns in =n take no suffix in the Dative Plural.

51. *To this Declension belong*

(*a*) Masculine and Neuter nouns in =el, =en, =er, and diminutives in =chen and =lein:

> der Himmel, sky; der Boden, ground; das Mädchen, girl.

N.B. Nine Masculines in =e are declined as if the Nom. Sing. ended in =en:

Buchstabe, Friede, Funke, Glaube, Name,   letter, peace, spark, faith, name,
Gedanke, Haufe, Wille, Same.   thought, heap, will, seed.

Gen. Sing. Buchstabens, Friedens, Funkens, etc.; all other cases, Buchstaben, Frieden, Funken, etc.

Note also der Fels, des Felsens; all other cases, Felsen; and das Herz, Acc. Herz, Gen. Herzens; all other cases, Herzen.

(*b*) Neuters with prefix Ge= and suffix =e:
> das Gebirge, mountain-range.

(*c*) die Mutter, mother; die Tochter, daughter; der Käse, cheese.

> Gen. Sing. der Mutter,   der Tochter,   des Käses.
> Nom. Pl. die Mütter,   die Töchter,   die Käse.

52. *The vowel does not modify in the Plural,* except in the Masculines:

Ofen, Sattel, Mantel,	stove, saddle, cloak,
Vogel, Schnabel, Handel,	bird, beak, business,
Nagel, Hammer, Mangel, Faden,	nail, hammer, want, thread,
Garten, Boden, Apfel, Laden,	garden, ground, apple, shop,
Acker, Hafen, Graben, Schaden,	field, haven, ditch, damage,
Vater, Bruder, Schwager,	father, brother, brother-in-law,

and the Neuter das Kloster, convent.

Pl. Öfen, Sättel, etc.

53.

		train	hand	desk
Sing.	N.	der Zug	die Hand	das Pult
	A.	den Zug	die Hand	das Pult
	G.	des Zug=es	der Hand	des Pult=es
	D.	dem Zug=e	der Hand	dem Pult=e
Plur.	N. & A.	die Züg=e	die Händ=e	die Pult=e
	G.	der Züg=e	der Händ=e	der Pult=e
	D.	den Züg=en	den Hände=n	den Pult=en.

Note. The e of the Gen. and Dat. Sing. is optional; but

(i) after a sibilant (s, ß, sch, z) or st, the Gen. must end in =es : der Schuß, Schuss=es; der Herbst, Herbst=es.

(ii) the e is usually dropped in nouns with an unstressed suffix; des Königs, dem König(e); des Jünglings, dem Jüngling(e).

54. *To this Declension belong*

(*a*) The bulk of the Masculines; i.e.

    (i) Monosyllabics, *usually with Umlaut in Pl.* Der Sohn, son, die Söhne; der Rock, coat, die Röcke.

    (ii) Masc. (and Neut.) nouns formed of Prefix + Verb-stem without suffix. *Masculines modify, Neuters do not.* Der Vertrag, treaty, die Verträge; das Gebot, commandment, die Gebote.

(iii) Masculines of more than one syllable not included in the other Declensions, especially those in -ich, -ig, -ing, -ling. *These do not modify.* Der Kranich, crane, Kraniche; der Abend, evening, die Abende; der Monat, month; der Amboß, anvil.

(*b*) All nouns in -nis and -sal. *These do not modify.* Note the doubling of the ß before a termination: das Zeugnis, testimonial, des Zeugnisses, die Zeugnisse.

(*c*) Some 40 Neuter monosyllabics, *none of which modify*:

Meer, Salz, Schiff, Boot,	sea, salt, ship, boat,
Netz, Beil, Pfund, Brot,	net, axe, pound, loaf,
Pferd, Roß, Fell, Haar,	horse, horse, skin, hair,
Reh, Schaf, Fest, Jahr,	deer, sheep, feast, year,
Reich, Recht, Knie, Bein,	realm, right, knee, leg,
Seil, Tau, Zelt, Schwein,	rope, cable, tent, pig,
Heft, Pult, Werk, Spiel,	book, desk, work, game,
Kreuz, Mal, Tor, Ziel,	cross, mark, gate, aim,
Band, Öl, Gift, Gas,	bond, oil, poison, gas,
Ding, Zeug, Stück, Maß.	thing, stuff, piece, measure.

(*d*) Some 35 Feminine monosyllabics, *all of which modify*:

Kraft, Faust, Macht, Hand,	power, fist, might, hand,
Lust, Axt, Bank, Wand,	desire, axe, bench, wall,
Kuh, Angst, Magd, Braut,	cow, fear, maid, bride,
Laus, Maus, Gans, Haut,	louse, mouse, goose, skin,
Not, Naht, Schnur, *-kunft,	need, stitch, string, coming,
Sau, Wurst, Kunst, Zunft,	sow, sausage, art, guild,
Stadt, Nacht, Gruft,	town, night, vault,
Nuß, Frucht, Luft.	nut, fruit, air.

* In compounds; e.g. Ankunft, arrival.

55. *The following monosyllabic Masculines do not modify:*

Aft, Taft, Laut, Hall,	act, bar (music), sound, sound,
Stoff, Schuft, Druck, Knall,	stuff, rogue, pressure, report,
Huf, Schuh, Arm, Hund,	hoof, shoe, arm, dog,
Dachs, Lachs, Hauch, Mund,	badger, salmon, breath, mouth,
Mond, Tag, Aar,	moon, day, eagle,
Horst, Punkt, Grad,	eyrie, point, degree,
Dolch, Dom, Star,	dagger, cathedral, starling,
Halm, Gau, Pfad.	stalk, district, path.

Six Masculine dissyllabics:	
Besuch, Gesuch, Versuch,	visit, request, attempt,
Erfolg, Gemahl, Verlust.	success, husband, loss.

56.   THIRD DECLENSION.

		house	error	wood
Sing.	N.	das Haus	der Irrtum	der Wald
	A.	das Haus	den Irrtum	den Wald
	G.	des Haus=es	des Irrtum=s	des Wald=es
	D.	dem Haus(e)	dem Irrtum	dem Wald(e)
Plur.	N. & A.	die Häus=er	die Irrtüm=er	die Wäld=er
	G.	der Häus=er	der Irrtüm=er	der Wäld=er
	D.	den Häus=ern	den Irrtüm=ern	den Wäld=ern

57. *To this Declension belong*

(*a*) All Neuter monosyllabics, except those of the Second Declension.

(*b*) Seven compounds of Ge=: das Gehalt, salary; das Gemach, room; das Gemüt, temperament; das Geschlecht, race, sex; das Gesicht, face; das Gespenst, ghost; das Gewand, robe.

(*c*) Masculines and Neuters in =tum: e.g. der Reichtum, riches; das Altertum, antiquity; das Eigentum, property.

(N.B. With the exception of Irrtum and Reichtum, all nouns in =tum are neuter.)

(*d*) Seven Masculine monosyllabics:

Geiſt, Gott, Leib, Mann,	spirit, God, body, man,
Wald, Wurm, Rand,	wood, worm, edge,

and der Vormund, guardian.

Der Ort, place, has plural Örter or Orte.

58.   FOURTH (WEAK) DECLENSION.

	lion	hero	clock	rose
Sing. N.	der Löwe	der Held	die Uhr	die Roſe
A.	den Löwe⸗n	den Held⸗en	die Uhr	die Roſe
G.	des Löwe⸗n	des Held⸗en	der Uhr	der Roſe
D.	dem Löwe⸗n	dem Held⸗en	der Uhr	der Roſe

Plur.

N.& A.	die ⎫	die ⎫	die ⎫	die ⎫
G.	der ⎬ Löwe⸗n	der ⎬ Held⸗en	der ⎬ Uhr⸗en	der ⎬ Roſe⸗n.
D.	den ⎭	den ⎭	den ⎭	den ⎭

Note. Feminines in ⸗in double the n in the plural: die Herrin, mistress, Herrin⸗nen.

59. *To this Declension belong*

(*a*) All Masculines in ⸗e, except those in §51: e.g. der Bote, messenger; der Erbe, heir; der Rieſe, giant; der Preuße, Prussian.

(*b*) Twenty Masculine monosyllabics, which formerly ended in ⸗e:

Ochs, Hirt, Menſch,	ox, herdsman, man,
Graf, Held, Herr,	count, hero, lord,
Fürſt, Prinz, Geck,	prince, prince, fop,
Spatz, Fink, Bär,	sparrow, finch, bear,
Ahn, Schenk, Chriſt, Mohr,	ancestor, butler, Christian, Moor,
Burſch, Lump, Narr, Tor.	fellow, rascal, fool, fool.

And the polysyllabics

Vorfahr, *Oberſt, Schultheiß,	ancestor, colonel, mayor,
Steinmetz, Hageſtolz.	mason, bachelor.

   * = der Oberſte, the highest (officer in the regiment).

(c) Some Masculines of foreign origin; see §§ 66 sqq.

(d) All Feminine monosyllabics not included in the Second Declension; see §54 (d).

The most important are:

Art, Form, Zahl,	kind, form, number,
Welt, Zeit, Uhr,	world, time, clock,
Schuld, Last, Qual,	debt, burden, torment,
Post, Bahn, Spur,	post, way, track,
Pflicht, Tat, Wahl,	duty, deed, election,
Frau, Schar, Schlacht,	woman, host, battle,
Burg, Tür, Tracht,	castle, door, costume,
Schrift, Fahrt, Flut,	writing, journey, flood,
Bucht, Schlucht, Brut.	bight, ravine, brood.

(e) All Feminine polysyllabics, except

(i) those in -nis and -sal. Pl. -nisse, -sale.

(ii) Mutter and Tochter. Pl. Mütter, Töchter.

60.   NOUNS OF MIXED DECLENSION.

The following nouns are strong in the singular and weak in the plural:

der Dorn	thorn	der Strahl	ray
Firn	glacier	Untertan	subject
Gevatter	godfather	Vetter	cousin
Lorbeer	laurel	Zins	interest
Mast	mast		
Nachbar	neighbour	das Auge	eye
Pantoffel	slipper	Bett	bed
Schmerz	pain	Ende	end
See	lake	Hemd	shirt
Staat	state	Leib	pain
Stachel	sting	Ohr	ear.

Der Bauer, peasant, and der Bayer, Bavarian, form Gen. Sing. Bauers or Bauern; Bayers or Bayern; and Nom. Pl. Bauern, Bayern.

Der Sporn, spur, is strong in the sing. but forms an irregular plural, die Sporen. Its compound Heißsporn, hotspur, has Heißsporne.

61. DOUBLE PLURAL FORMS.

The most important are:

der Band	volume	Bände	volumes		
das Band	ribbon, fetter	Bänder	ribbons	Bande	fetters
die Bank	bench, bank (for money)	Bänke	benches	Banken	banks
der Bauer	peasant	Bauern	peasants		
der (das) Bauer	cage	Bauer	cages		
das Gesicht	face, vision	Gesichte	visions	Gesichter	faces
der Bogen	arch, etc.	Bögen	arches, bows	Bogen	sheets of paper
der Laden	shop, shutter	Läden	shops	Laden	shutters
der Schild	shield	Schilde			
das Schild	signboard	Schilder			
das Wort	word	Wörter	disconnected words	Worte	connected words.

62. NOUNS WITH ONLY ONE NUMBER.

Some nouns have no singular form; such are Leute, people; Eltern, parents; Beinkleider, trousers; Molken, curds and whey; Masern, measles; Röteln, German measles; Kosten (Unkosten) expenses.

Many have no plural form, and to express the meaning of certain English plurals, we must borrow from cognate or derivative words, e.g.

der Bau	building	die Bauten
der Bund	alliance	Bündnisse
das Erbe	heritage	Erbschaften
der Friede	peace	Friedensverträge

die Gunst	favour	Gunstbezeugungen
das Lob	praise	Lobsprüche
der Mord	murder	Mordtaten
der Rat	counsel	Ratschläge
der Raub	robbery	Raubfälle
der Streit	quarrel	Streitigkeiten
der Tod	death	Todesfälle, Todesarten.

Der Dank, thanks, is used only in the singular.

63.   DECLENSION OF FOREIGN NOUNS.

The majority of these nouns are assimilated to the German language, and belong to one or other of the ordinary declensions; many, however, have not been assimilated, and are declined as in § 73.

I. *ASSIMILATED NOUNS.*

64. Feminines form their plural in ‑en or ‑n:

die Auktion, auction, Auktion‑en.   die Krise, crisis, Krise‑n.
die Armee, army, Armee‑n.   die Zigarre, cigar, Zigarre‑n.

N.B.   Final a is elided: die Primadonna. Pl. Primadonn‑en.

65. Masculines and Neuters in ‑el, ‑er, are of the First Declension if accented on the penultimate:

der Kaiser	emperor	Pl. Kaiser
der Krater	crater	Krater
das Meter	metre	Meter
der Revolver	revolver	Revolver
das Theater	theatre	Theater
das Barometer	barometer	Barometer.

But der Charakter   des Charakters   die Charaktére
der Muskel   des Muskels   die Muskeln.

66. Masculine Nouns accented on the last syllable belong to the Weak Declension if (i) they denote persons, *and* (ii) they are derived either from the Greek or from Latin or Romance participles.

Nouns derived from the Greek:

ber Monarch, monarch	ber Despot, despot
Gymnaſt, gymnast	Aſtrolog, astrologer
Poliziſt, policeman	Ökonom, steward
Paraſit, parasite	Photograph, photographer
Demokrat, democrat	Stenograph, shorthand-writer
Israelit, Israelite	Tyrann, tyrant.

All other cases: Monarchen, Gymnaſten, Poliziſten, uſw.

Note that nouns similar in form, but denoting things without life, belong to the Second Declension:

ber Dialog, dialogue; ber Katalog, catalogue. Pl. Dialoge, Kataloge.

67. *Nouns derived from Participles:*

ber Abiturient	candidate for matriculation	abituriens
Dirigent	conductor of orchestra	dirigens
Expreß	express	expressus
Kanbibat	candidate	candidatus
Konfirmanb	candidate for confirmation	confirmandus
Paſſant	passer-by, casual customer	*Fr.* passant
Präfekt	prefect	praefectus
Prälat	prelate	praelatus
Profoß	provost-marshal	propositus
Rekrut	recruit	*Fr.* recrue
Solbat	soldier	*Ital.* soldato (= paid)
Student	student	studens.

All other cases: Abiturienten, Dirigenten, Expreſſen, Kanbibaten, uſw.

68. Also

ber Chriſt, Christian	ber Faſan, pheasant	ber Planet, planet
Diamant, diamond	Huſar, Hussar	Prinz, prince
Elefant, elephant	Kroat, Croatian	Ulan, Uhlan.

Der Kamerad, comrade, is also weak, being derived from the
Spanish *camarada* (fem.), "a roomful," and so "a room-mate."
Rekrut was also originally feminine, from French *recrue*.

**69. All other Masculines and Neuters stressed on the last
syllable** are of the Second Declension:

der General, general	⸗ale or ⸗äle	der Likör, liqueur	⸗öre
Offizier, officer	⸗iere	Katalog, catalogue	⸗oge
Altar, altar	⸗are or ⸗äre	Palast, palace	⸗äste
Missionär, missionary	⸗äre	Roman, novel	⸗ane
Chauffeur, chauffeur	⸗eure	Kongreß, congress	⸗esse.

Similarly

das Abjektiv, adjective   der Major, major
der Apparat, apparatus   der Omnibus, omnibus
das Atom, atom   (⸗busses, ⸗busse)
das Automobil, motor   der Prozeß, lawsuit
das Billett, ticket   das Skelett, skeleton
der Championat, championship   das System, system
der Friseur, barber   das Telegramm, telegram
das Instrument, instrument   das Telephon, telephone
der Kapitän, captain   der Teleskop, telescope
der Kaplan, chaplain (⸗äne)   das Vestibül, vestibule.

Very few nouns of this type modify in the plural.

70. N.B. das Hospital, das Spital, hospital; die Hospitäler,
         Spitäler.
        das Regiment, regiment; Regimenter.

71. Masculines and Neuters stressed on the penultimate
and not ending in ⸗el or ⸗er are strong in the singular and
weak in the plural, e.g. der Dóktor, des Dóktors, die Doktóren.

Similarly der Pástor, der Proféssor, der Prátor, der Zénsor, der
Kónsul (pl. die Konsúln).

Neuters, in forming the plural, shed the foreign termination
before adding ⸗en:

das Drama	des Dramas	die Dram⸗en
das Epos	des Epos	die Ep⸗en
das Museum	des Museums	die Muse⸗en
das Individuum	des Individuums	die Individu⸗en.

72. The following Neuters are, irregularly, strong in the sing.
and weak in the plural:

Adverb, Kapital, Mineral, Juwel, Psalm, Insekt, Verb.

Gen. Adverbs, Kapitals, usw.

Pl. Adverbien, Kapitalien, Mineralien, Juwelen, Psalmen, Insekten,
Verben.

Das Kleinod, jewel, though a pure Germanic word, forms pl.
Kleinódien.

II. *Nouns not Assimilated.*

73. This class includes, amongst others, all foreign nouns
ending in a vowel sound other than a or e. They form the
plural by adding ⸗s, though in a few cases a native plural
not ending in ⸗s is retained, e.g. das Conto, account, pl.
Contos or Conti. Masculines and Neuters add ⸗s in the
Gen. Sing.

Sing.	N.	der Sport	der Leutnant	die Bill
	A.	den Sport	den Leutnant	die Bill
	G.	des Sports	des Leutnants	der Bill
	D.	dem Sport	dem Leutnant	der Bill

Plur.	N. & A.	die ⎫	die ⎫	die ⎫
	G.	der ⎬ Sports	der ⎬ Leutnants	der ⎬ Bills.
	D.	den ⎭	den ⎭	den ⎭

Similarly der Jockey, der Park, der Klub, der Pudding, der Strike,
der Ballon (balő), der Banquier (bäkje), der Toreador, der Torpedo;
and the German noun der Uhu (screech-owl), des Uhus, die Uhus.

N.B. das Bureau, die Lady form pl. die Bureaus, die Ladys.

Declension of Proper Nouns
(Deflination der Eigennamen).

74. Proper Names of Persons, when used with the Article, are uninflected:

die Reden des Cicero, the speeches of Cicero.

die Schuhe der kleinen Bertha, little Bertha's shoes.

Used without the Article, they take *s* in the Genitive; those in s, g, z take *ens* or apostrophe; feminines in e add *ns*:

Karls Buch, Goethes Werke, Berthas Schuhe; Hansens Eltern, Hans' Pult; Mariens Feder.

But classical names in s do not add *ens*. They shew the Genitive either by means of an apostrophe or by a preceding Definite Article:

Sophokles' Tragödien, or
die Tragödien des Sophokles } Sophocles' tragedies.

75. Proper Names of Places, if regularly used with the Article, are declined like common nouns; e.g.

N.	der Vesuv	die Schweiz	die Niederlande
A.	den Vesuv	die Schweiz	die Niederlande
G.	des Vesuvs	der Schweiz	der Niederlande
D.	dem Vesuv	der Schweiz	den Niederlanden.

76. Those regularly used without the Article mark the Gen. Sing. by adding *s*, but do not inflect other cases; e.g.

die Flüsse Deutschlands, Germany's rivers, the rivers of Germany; die Wälle Magdeburgs, the walls of Magdeburg; in Hamburg, in Hamburg. But these nouns are uninflected after the Article: die Wälle des festen Magdeburg.

Place-names in s, g, z cannot form a Genitive. They mark the case by means of von or a noun in apposition:

die Einwohner von Mainz, or die Einwohner der Stadt Mainz, the inhabitants of Mainz.

NOUNS IN APPOSITION (die Appoſition).

77. Nouns in Apposition agree in case:

Kennen Sie meinen Freund, den Bürgermeiſter?
Do you know my friend the mayor?
Sagen Sie das meinem Herrn, dem Grafen!
Tell that to my master, the count.

78. In the case of a double name, or of a name preceded by
a title without the Definite Article, the latter word alone
is inflected:

Guſtav Adolfs Page, Gustavus Adolphus' page.
König Friedrichs Schloß, King Frederick's palace.

79. After Article + Title, or Article + Adjective, the proper
name is uninflected:

Das Schloß des Königs Friedrich; das Schloß des großen
Friedrich. But das Schloß Friedrichs des Großen, since the Article
does not precede.

80. But Herr (Mr.) is always declined:

Herrn Meyers Hut, or der Hut des Herrn Meyer.
Mr. Meyer's hat.

81. German sometimes uses Apposition where English has the
Genitive:

Die Stadt London, the city *of* London;
das Königreich Großbritannien, the kingdom *of* Great Britain;
Cf. die Familie Robinſon, the Robinson family.

82. After als care is sometimes required:

Ich ſage es dir, als ein Freund.
I tell you, as *a friend would tell you.*

Ich ſage es dir, als einem Freunde.
I tell you, as *one tells a friend.*

THE CASES (der Kasus, pl. die Kasus).

THE NOMINATIVE (der Nominativ).

83. The Nominative is used

(*a*) as **Subject** of a verb:

Die Zeit vergeht. Time flies.

(*b*) as a **Vocative**:

O holber Friede, steig' hernieder!

Sweet Peace, come down to earth.

(*c*) as **Predicative Noun** after sein, werden, bleiben, heißen, etc.:

Wär' ich besonnen, hieß' ich nicht der Tell.

My name would not be Tell, if I were prudent.

See §§ 84 (*c*), 391 (*a*).

THE ACCUSATIVE (der Affusativ).

84. The Accusative is used

(*a*) after certain **Prepositions**; see § 415 sqq.

(*b*) as **Direct Object** of a transitive verb:

Sie kämmt ihr goldenes Haar.

She combs her golden hair.

(*c*) as **Second Object** after a verb governing two accusatives.
These verbs are of two kinds:

(i) Some take two accusatives, denoting different objects:

Er lehrt mich Deutsch. He teaches me German.

Ich muß dich eins fragen. I must ask you one question.

Das Buch hat mich eine Mark gekostet.

The book cost me one mark.

With bitten and fragen, only a pronoun can stand in the
accusative as the second object; see § 391 (*d*).

(ii) Some take two accusatives, referring to the same object;
e.g. heißen, call; nennen, name; schelten, scold; schimpfen, scold;
taufen, dub.

Er nannte mich seinen Freund.   He called me his friend.

In this case the second object is predicative.

The passive of a verb of this class takes a predicate in the nominative.

85. N.B. (i) The Second Object may be a Predicative Adjective:

Er fühlte sich glücklich.   He felt happy.

Der Wirt schenkte das Glas voll.   The host filled the glass full.

Er hat sich satt gegessen.   He has eaten his fill.

In many such cases the adjective has become a separable prefix:

los=machen, los=lassen, frei=lassen, to release; frei=sprechen, acquit; tot=schießen, shoot (dead); sich tot ärgern, to be mortally angry.

See § 391 (a).

86. N.B. (ii) The Second Object is expressed

(i) by als + Predicative Noun, after betrachten (consider) ansehen (regard), anerkennen (recognise):

> Er betrachtet Sie als einen Wohltäter.
> He regards you as a benefactor.

Passively: Sie werden als ein Wohltäter betrachtet.

(ii) by zu + Dative, after machen (make), ernennen (appoint), wählen (elect), krönen (crown):

> Die Räuber wählten Karl Moor zu ihrem Hauptmann.
> The brigands elected K. M. to be their chief.

Passively: Er wurde zum Hauptmann gewählt.

(iii) by für + Accusative, after halten, erklären (consider):

> Ich hielt Sie für einen ehrlichen Mann.
> I thought you an honest man.

3-2

87. (*d*) **as Cognate Accusative** after an intransitive verb :

Er lebt ein elendes Leben. He lives a wretched life.

Er ist einen rühmlichen Tod gestorben.
He has died a glorious death.

Gehe deinen Weg! Go thy way.

Cf. Rache schnauben, to breathe vengeance.

88. (*e*) **as Accusative Absolute** :

Zu Dionys, dem Tyrannen, schlich
Damon, den Dolch im Gewande.

Towards Dionysius the tyrant crept Damon, with his
dagger in his robe.

This accusative is usually explained as the object of a
suppressed participle habend.

89. (*f*) **Adverbially** :

(i) as a measure of time, weight, space :

Es regnete drei Stunden lang. It rained for three hours.
Wir marschierten 20 Kilometer.
We marched 20 kilometres.

(ii) of time, answering the question "when?" :

Den andern Tag kam er zurück. Next day he returned.

This use is to be distinguished from the Genitive of time,
which refers to a repeated or habitual act :

Sonntags geht man in die Kirche.
On *Sundays* we go to church.

but   Sonntag gehen wir in die Kirche.
We shall go to church *next Sunday*.

The Genitive Case (der Genitiv).

90. A noun (or pronoun) in the Genitive may depend on
another noun; it may be governed by a verb, an adjective, or a preposition; or it may be used independently.

91. The **Genitive depending on a Noun** may be

Possessive: Der Ring des Polykrates.
The ring of Polycrates.

Subjective: Goethes Werke. Goethe's Works.

Objective: Der Verlust dieses Geldes.
The loss of this money.

Partitive: Eine Flasche des besten Weins.
A bottle of the best wine.

Descriptive: Ein Mann von Ihrem Charakter.
A man of your character.

92. Many **Verbs** govern the Genitive, but the tendency in modern German is to substitute an Accusative or a prepositional phrase.

Bedürfen, need; entbehren, lack; erwähnen, mention; pflegen, tend; schonen, spare; vergessen, forget, take an Accusative.

Frohlocken, exult, and spotten, mock, take über with the Acc.

Harren and warten, wait, take auf with Acc.

Mein Haus entbehrt des Vaters. (Schiller.)
My house is without its master.
Ich kann Sie nicht entbehren. I cannot do without you.

93. Some Verbs take an **Acc. of the Person** and a **Gen. of the Thing:**

anklagen, accuse	erinnern, remind (also with an)
beschuldigen, „	freisprechen, acquit
zeihen, „	überführen, convict
berauben, rob	würdigen, deem worthy
entlasten, unburden	überzeugen, convince (also with von).

Die Räuber entlasteten uns unsres Geldes.
The brigands relieved us of our money.

94. Many **Reflexive Verbs** take a Gen.:

ſich annehmen, take interest in
  bebenken, remember
  bebienen, make use of
  freuen, rejoice in
  bemächtigen, get possession of
  beſinnen, think of (also with auf)

ſich enthalten, refrain from
  erbarmen, take pity on
  erfreuen, enjoy
  rühmen, boast of
  ſchämen, be ashamed of
  verſichern, make sure of.

   Herr, erbarme bich unſer! Lord, have mercy upon us.
   Er rühmte ſich ſeiner Muskeln. He boasted of his muscles.

95. The following **Adjectives** govern the Gen.:

  (*Separation*): frei, free; los, loose; lebig, bar, free, clear of.
  (*Fulness and want*): voll, full; ſatt, satisfied; bebürftig, in need of.

  (*With verbal force*):

      anſichtig, in sight of   gewiß, sure of
      bewußt, conscious   mächtig, master
      eingebenk, mindful   ſchulbig, guilty
      fähig, capable   unſchulbig, innocent
      gewahr, aware   teilhaft, partner.
      gewohnt, accustomed

Also wert, würbig, worthy; froh, glad; müde, weary.

96. *Note.* Gewahr, gewohnt, los, müde, ſatt also govern the Acc.
  Wert (used of money-value) and ſchulbig (meaning 'indebted') always take the Acc.
  Bewußt takes a Refl. Pronoun in the Dat. besides the Gen.

    Ich bin mir keines Verbrechens bewußt.
    I am not conscious of any crime.
    Ich bin bieses Verbrechens ſchulbig.
    I am guilty of this crime.
  But Ich bin Ihnen eine Mark ſchulbig.   I owe you one mark.
    Er iſt aller Ehre wert. He is worthy of all praise.
  But Es iſt keinen Heller wert. It is not worth a cent.

97. For **Prepositions** governing the Gen. see § 452.

98. The Gen. used **independently** may be either

(*a*) a Predicate after ſein:

Ich bin der Meinung. I am of the opinion.

Sei guten Mutes! Be of good courage.

Wir waren (lauter) guter Dinge. We were in high spirits.

or (*b*) Adverbial:

Schnellen Schritts müßt ihr vorüber eilen.
With a quick step you must hasten past.

Nach Uri fahr' ich stehenden Fußes.
Without delay I will set out for Uri.

Gehe deines Weges! Go thy way.

Hungers ſterben, to die of hunger; rechts und links, right
and left; Sonntags, on Sundays; des Nachts, o'nights.

99. The **Saxon Genitive** resembles the English equivalent
construction:

das Haus meines Vaters ⎱
meines Vaters Haus   ⎰ my father's house.

die Gunſt der Götter ⎱
der Götter Gunſt   ⎰ the favour of the gods.

In modern German the Saxon genitive is used almost ex-
clusively to denote possession. A century ago, and in poetry,
it was far more widely used. Where Schiller wrote Aegyptens
König, der Griechen Stämme, the modern prose equivalents would
be der König von Aegypten, die Stämme der Griechen.

100. *Note.* A succession of dependent genitives should be
avoided by the use of von, a Saxon genitive, or a compound noun. Instead of

die Mutter der Frau meines Bruders,

say die Mutter von meines Bruders Frau,

or die Mutter von der Frau meines Bruders.

'The fate of the inhabitants of the town' is translated:

das Schicksal der Stadtbewohner,

or das Schicksal von den Bewohnern der Stadt.

101. 𝔙𝔬𝔫 is used instead of the Genitive

(*a*) *after* frei, los, rein, leer:

> Frei von Schuld.   Free of guilt.

(*b*) *partitively, after numerals, superlatives and pronouns*, though here the Genitive is also correct:

> Zwei von meinen Freunden.   Two friends of mine.
> Das beste von meinen Büchern.   The best of my books.
> Welches von diesen Büchern?   Which of these books?
> Einer von Ihnen muß gehen.   One of you must go.

(*c*) *to show origin, material, quality:*

> Der Kaufmann von Venedig.   The merchant of Venice.
> Ein Becher von Gold.   A golden cup.
> Ein Mann von Charakter.   A man of character.

(*d*) *after titles of rank*, usually denoting the territory governed:

> Der König von Spanien.   The King of Spain.
> Der Graf von Egmont (also Graf Egmont).   Count Egmont.
> Der Oberbürgermeister von London.
> The Lord Mayor of London.

(*e*) to avoid a succession of genitives; see § 100, above.

102. The Genitive is not used

(*a*) *when the two nouns are really in Apposition :*

> Die Stadt Paris.   The city of Paris.
> Der Monat Mai.   The month of May.

When the second noun is a Gerund, it is expressed by zu + Infinitive:

> Die Kunst, zu malen.   The art of painting.

(*b*) *in dates, before the name of the month :*

> Am fünften November.   On the fifth of November.

(*c*) *after nouns of weight, measure*, etc.:

        Ein Zentner Kartoffeln.   A hundredweight of potatoes.

        Ein Meter Tuch.   A yard of cloth.

        Eine Flasche Wein.   A bottle of wine.

But when the second noun is defined, use the Genitive or von + Dat.: eine Flasche dieses Weins, von diesem Wein, von dem besten Wein, von unserm Wein.

When the second noun is qualified but not defined, von cannot be used:

        Er brachte eine Flasche guten Wein, or guten Weins;

    not eine Flasche von gutem Wein.

N.B. Masc. and Neut. nouns of measure, etc., take no plural ending: zwei Pfund Brot, zwei Fuß lang, zehn Grad Kälte. But zwei Ellen Tuch, vier Flaschen Wein. Mark is also invariable.

(*d*) *after several nouns with verbal meaning:*

        Die Furcht vor Gespenstern.   The fear of ghosts.

        Der Gedanke an die Zukunft.   The thought of the future.

        Die Liebe zum Vaterland or Vaterlandsliebe, patriotism;

    not die Liebe des Vaterlandes.

But 'the fear of God' is die Furcht Gottes.

THE DATIVE CASE (der Dativ).

103. The Dative is used

     (*a*) **After Prepositions**; see §§ 424—451.

104. (*b*) As the **Indirect Object** of transitive verbs, e.g.

bieten, offer	lassen, leave	reichen, pass
bringen, bring	leihen, lend	sagen, say
erlauben, allow	melden, announce	schenken, present
glauben, believe	raten, advise	zeigen, show.

Sagen Sie das meiner Frau!   Tell that to my wife.

Melden Sie mich Ihrem Herrn!   Announce me to your master.

Ich gab ihm einen guten Rat.   I gave him some good advice.

N.B. In the Passive the Indirect Object remains in the Dative:

> Ihm wurde ein guter Rat gegeben. He was given, etc.
> Mir ist gesagt worden. I have been told.

105. Note also that the contraries of some of the above verbs are constructed with the Dative:

rauben, rob	entziehen, withhold	nehmen, take away
verbieten, forbid	versagen, refuse	abraten, dissuade
verhehlen, conceal	borgen, borrow	stehlen, steal.

> Es raubt mir den Atem. It takes my breath away.
> Verhehle mir nicht die Wahrheit!
> Do not conceal the truth from me.

Verzeihen and vergeben (forgive) are used with a Dat. of the person, with or without an Acc. of the thing:

> Verzeihen Sie mir! Pardon me.
> Ich verzeihe Ihnen alles. I forgive you everything.

Nachahmen (imitate) takes a Dative of the person, or an Accusative of the thing:

> Er ahmt mir nach. He imitates me.
> Er ahmt meine Gebärden nach. He imitates my gestures.

106. (c) **After many Intransitive Verbs,** corresponding in some cases to English transitives; e.g.

begegnen, meet	gratulieren, congratulate	schaden, harm
danken, thank	helfen, help	schmeicheln, flatter
dienen, serve	mangeln, be wanting	trauen, trust
drohen, threaten	nahen, approach	trotzen, defy
fehlen, fail	nützen, be useful	ziemen, befit
folgen, follow	passen, fit	zürnen, be angry.
gleichen, resemble		

107. And after many compounds of Prefix + Intransitive Verb:

auffallen, strike	entsagen, renounce
gefallen, please	entgegengehen, go to meet
mißfallen, displease	entgegenkommen, come to meet
einfallen, occur	beistehen, help
ausweichen, avoid	gehorchen, obey
entfliehen ⎫	gehören, belong
entgehen ⎬ escape	widersprechen, contradict
entkommen ⎭	widerstehen, resist.
entsprechen, correspond	

Diese Arbeit gefällt mir nicht. This work does not please me.

Er widerspricht mir beständig. He is always contradicting me.

Er wird Ihren Wünschen entgegenkommen.

He will meet your wishes.

108. N.B. These verbs cannot be used in the Passive, except impersonally:

I was pleased by his behaviour. Mir gefiel sein Benehmen.

He was followed by his son. Ihm folgte sein Sohn.

The man can be helped. Dem Mann kann geholfen werden.

109. (*d*) After some Impersonal Verbs:

Es ekelt mir vor diesem Kerl. This fellow disgusts me.

Es fehlt (or mangelt) mir an Geld. I lack money.

Es graut (or schaudert) mir davor. It makes me shudder.

Es schwindelt mir ⎱
Mir schwindelt ⎰. My brain reels.

Es ist mir nicht wohl. I don't feel well.

Mir ist, als ob.... I feel as though....

Es geht mir gut. I am well.

Es tut mir leid; ......weh; ......wohl.

I am sorry; it hurts me; it does me good.

See §§ 307 to 310.

110. (*e*) In less close dependence on the verb, as **dativus commodi**, esp. with reflexives; or instead of a possessive adjective:

Er füllte mir das Glas. He filled my glass.

Er liegt mir vor den Füßen. He lies at my feet.

Er läßt sich ein Haus bauen. He is having a house built.

Der Strang ist mir entzwei; mach' mir ihn, Vater!
My bow-string is broken; mend it for me, father.

Note also the Ethic Dative:

Die Türken haben dir Säbels mit Diamanten besetzt.
The Turks have sabres—look you!—set with diamonds.

111. (*f*) **After many Adjectives**, whose English equivalents are generally followed by *to*; e.g.

bekannt, well-known	nützlich, useful
dienstbar, serviceable	schädlich, hurtful
ergeben, devoted	vorteilhaft, advantageous
notwendig, necessary	willkommen, welcome.
unentbehrlich, indispensable	

Dieses Geld ist mir unentbehrlich.
This money is indispensable to me.

Gleich and ähnlich come under this category:

Er sieht seinem Vater ganz ähnlich. He is just like his father.

An Adjective or Adverb modified by genug or zu takes a Dative of the person interested:

Diese Schuhe sind mir viel zu teuer.
These shoes are much too dear for me.

Dieses Zimmer ist mir (nicht) groß genug.
This room is (not) large enough for me.

Compare:

Es ist mir unmöglich, das Haus zu kaufen.
It is impossible *for me* to buy the house.

IV. ADJECTIVES

(das Abjektiv, pl. die Abjektive)

DECLENSION.

112. I. Adjectives of Fixed Declension.

These are divided into two groups, the Dieser-group and the Mein-group.

The Dieser-group comprises the Definite Article and

dieser, this;	jener, that;	welcher? which?
jeder, each;	mancher, many a;	solcher, such;
derjenige, that;	derselbe, the same;	aller, all.

113. They are declined:

	Singular			Plural
	M.	F.	N.	all genders
N.	dies-er	dies-e	dies-es	dies-e
A.	dies-en	dies-e	dies-es	dies-e
G.	dies-es	dies-er	dies-es	dies-er
D.	dies-em	dies-er	dies-em	dies-en.

114. The Mein-group comprises the Indefinite Article, kein, and the Possessive Adjectives

mein, my;	dein, thy;	sein, his;	ihr, her;
unser, our;	euer, your;	ihr, their;	Ihr, your.

115. They are declined:

	M.	F.	N.	Plural
N.	mein	mein-e	mein	mein-e
A.	mein-en	mein-e	mein	mein-e
G.	mein-es	mein-er	mein-es	mein-er
D.	mein-em	mein-er	mein-em	mein-en.

Note that the -er in unser, euer, is part of the stem. They are therefore declined unser, unsere, unser; A. unseren, unsere, unser, etc.

116. II. Adjectives of Variable Declension.

This term is applied to all adjectives, other than those referred to in §112 and §114, and the cardinal numbers.

117. These may be uninflected, as when used predicatively or when they follow their noun:

Das Kind war tot.	The child was dead.
Es war ein König in Thule,	There was a king in Thule,
Gar treu bis an das Grab.	Faithful even to the grave.

118. When they come before the noun, their declension varies according as they are preceded by an adjective of fixed declension or not.

119. Strong Declension.

When no adjective of fixed declension precedes, the adjective takes the same terminations as dieser. But in the Genitive Sing. masculine and neuter, to avoid the repetition of the -es-ending, -en is substituted. Thus:

N. kalt-er Stahl	warm-e Luft	alt-es Holz	gut-e Leute
A. kalt-en Stahl	warm-e Luft	alt-es Holz	gut-e Leute
G. kalt-en Stahles	warm-er Luft	alt-en Holzes	gut-er Leute
D. kalt-em Stahle	warm-er Luft	alt-em Holze	gut-en Leuten.

120. Weak Declension.

When preceded by an adjective of fixed declension, the attributive adjective takes the weak ending, except where the adjective of fixed declension has no ending at all, i.e. in the Nom. Sing. masc. and the Nom. and Acc. Sing. neuter of ein, mein, etc. Thus there is always one, and only one, strong ending.

121. The weak endings are:

	M.	F.	N.	Pl.
N.	ꞏe	ꞏe	ꞏe	ꞏen
A.	ꞏen	ꞏe	ꞏe	ꞏen
G.	ꞏen	ꞏen	ꞏen	ꞏen
D.	ꞏen	ꞏen	ꞏen	ꞏen.

122. Adjective preceded by biefer, **etc. (Weak Declension.)**

Singular.

N.	ber altꞏe Mann	bie golbnꞏe Uhr	bas neuꞏe Haus
A.	ben altꞏen Mann	bie golbnꞏe Uhr	bas neuꞏe Haus
G.	bes altꞏen Mannes	ber golbnꞏen Uhr	bes neuꞏen Haufes
D.	bem altꞏen Manne	ber golbnꞏen Uhr	bem neuꞏen Haufe

Plural.

N. & A.	bie altꞏen Männer	golbnꞏen Uhren	neuꞏen Häufer
G.	ber altꞏen Männer	golbnꞏen Uhren	neuꞏen Häufer
D.	ben altꞏen Männern	golbnꞏen Uhren	neuꞏen Häufern

Derjenige and berfelbe are declined as ber + Adjective:

Sing.	N.	berfelbe	biefelbe	basfelbe	Pl.	biefelben
	A.	benfelben	biefelbe	basfelbe		biefelben
	G.	besfelben	berfelben	besfelben		berfelben
	D.	bemfelben	berfelben	bemfelben		benfelben.

123. Adjective preceded by mein, **etc. (Mixed Declension.)**
(Feminine as in § 122.)

Sing.	N.	mein altꞏer Freund	unfer kleinꞏes Haus
	A.	meinen altꞏen Freund	unfer kleinꞏes Haus
	G.	meines altꞏen Freundes	unferes kleinꞏen Haufes
	D.	meinem altꞏen Freunde	unferem kleinꞏen Haufe
Pl.	N. & A.	meine altꞏen Freunde	unfere kleinꞏen Häufer
	G.	meiner altꞏen Freunde	unferer kleinꞏen Häufer
	D.	meinen altꞏen Freunden	unferen kleinꞏen Häufern.

Two or more adjectives qualifying the same noun take the same ending: ein großer, ftarfer Mann ; ber arme, alte König.

NOTES ON THE DECLENSION OF ADJECTIVES.

124. (*a*) The presence or absence of a noun does not affect
the declension of the adjective:

Wir haben zwei Autos, ein großes und ein kleines.
We have two cars, a large one and a small one.

125. (*b*) Some adjectives are frequently used as nouns, e.g.

der Fremde, stranger	der Deutsche, German
der Gelehrte, scholar	der Gefangene, prisoner
der Reisende, traveller	der Alte, old man
der Gesandte, ambassador	der Angeklagte, accused person.

Ein Fremder, ein Deutscher, etc.
Zwei Reisende, drei Gefangene, etc.

126. (*c*) Note the neuter expressions das Schöne, that which
is beautiful, beauty; das Neue, that which is new,
novelty; das Wichtigste, the main thing, etc.

127. (*d*) In such expressions as etwas Gutes, viel Gutes, wenig
Gutes, the ∕es is really a genitive ending; cf. *quelque
chose de bon, aliquid boni.* Nevertheless it changes to
∕em in the dative: zu nichts Gutem, for no good
purpose.

128. (*e*) After einige, some, etliche, some, viele, many, wenige,
few, mehrere, several, verschiedene, various, the ending
is usually ∕e in the nom. and acc. plural, ∕en in the
gen. and dat.:

N. & A. viele klein∕e Tiere
G. vieler klein∕en Tiere
D. vielen klein∕en Tieren.

129. (*f*) When a Personal Pronoun is followed by Adj. +
Noun, the mixed declension is used: ich armer Mann;
du armes Kind; ihr armen Leute. But we can say
either ihr Deutsche, or ihr Deutschen, you Germans.

130. (*g*) Adjectives in ⸗el, ⸗en usually, those in ⸗er occasionally, drop the e of the stem before the endings ⸗e, ⸗er, ⸗es: ein edler Mann, eine ebne Fläche, eine beßre Welt.

Those in ⸗el and ⸗er add ⸗m, ⸗n, instead of ⸗em, ⸗en: bei heiterm Wetter, in bright weather; einen edeln Mann, a noble man.

But with adjectives in ⸗er it is correct to retain both the stem ⸗e and that of the ending: unsere, unseres, unserem.

131. (*h*) Hoch, when inflected, becomes hoh⸗: ein hoher Berg; hohe Berge.

132. (*i*) All, followed by a demonstrative or possessive adjective, is undeclined in the singular and usually in the plural: all mein Geld, all my money; mit all meinem Gelde, with all my money; all diese Leute or alle diese Leute, all these people. Note that alle Schüler means *either* 'all schoolboys' *or* 'all the schoolboys'; all die Schüler means 'all *these* boys.'

133. (*j*) Indeclinable are
   (i) the cardinal numbers from zwei upwards; but see § 152.
   (ii) adjectives in ⸗lei; see § 162.
   (iii) adjectives in ⸗er formed from place-names: Münchner Bier, Munich beer; Schweizer Käse, Gruyère cheese; die Berliner Polizei, the Berlin police.

134. Other adjectives may be used without inflection, e.g. lauter, ganz, halb:
Halb Paris ist freudetrunken. Half Paris is wild with joy.
Er ist in ganz England bekannt. He is known in all England.

135. Distinguish between
laut, loud: mit lauter Stimme, with a loud voice;
lauter, pure: lauteres Wasser, pure water;
lauter (indecl.), sheer: lauter Unsinn, sheer nonsense. Das sind lauter Schurken, these fellows are a pack of rogues.

Comparison of Adjectives
(Komparation oder Steigerung).

136. The Comparative and Superlative are formed by adding
(respectively) ⸗er (⸗r) and ⸗eſt (⸗ſt) to the Positive:

reich	rich	reicher	reichſt
trübe	dim	trüber	trübſt
ſüß	sweet	ſüßer	ſüßeſt.

Adjectives ending in a dental stop or spirant, d, t, ß, ſch, z,
form the Superlative in ⸗eſt: geſund, healthy, geſundeſt; heiß, hot,
heißeſt.

Participles in ⸗d and ⸗t add ⸗eſt only when the accent is on
the last syllable:

	bekannt well-known	bekannter	bekannteſt;
but	raſend furious	raſender	raſendſt.

137. Adjectives in ⸗el, ⸗en, ⸗er, usually drop the stem ⸗e in the
Comparative but not in the Superlative:

edel	noble	edler	edelſt
verwegen	foolhardy	verwegner	verwegenſt.

138. Monosyllabic adjectives modify the stem vowels a, o, u:

lang	long	länger	längſt
kurz	short	kürzer	kürzeſt.

Exceptions:

(*a*) au-stems, e.g. blau, blue, blauer, blau(e)ſt.

(*b*)

brav	worthy	hohl	hollow	platt	flat	ſtolz	proud
bunt	gay	kahl	bald	raſch	quick	ſtumm	dumb
falſch	false	klar	clear	roh	raw	ſtumpf	blunt
flach	flat	lahm	lame	rund	round	toll	mad
froh	glad	matt	dull	ſanft	soft	voll	full
				ſchlank	slender	wahr	true.

139. The Superlative of the adjective is usually preceded by the Definite Article or a possessive adjective: ber höchſte Berg, the highest mountain; mein beſter Freunb, my best friend. Welcher von bieſen Jungen iſt ber älteſte? Which of these boys is the oldest?

140. Irregular Comparison.

groß	great	größer	größt
gut	good	beſſer	beſt
hoch	high	höher	höchſt
nahe	near	näher	nächſt
viel	much	mehr	meiſt
wenig	little	minber	minbeſt
		(weniger)	(wenigſt).

141. Adjectives lacking Positives:

(auß)	äußer	outer, exterior	äußerſt	outermost, extreme
(in)	inner	inner, interior	innerſt	inmost
(oben)	ober	upper	oberſt	highest
(unten)	unter	lower	unterſt	lowest
(hinten)	hinter	hinder	hinterſt	hindmost
(vorn)	vorber	(forward)	vorberſt	foremost.

Hinter and unter have developed into prepositions, as auß and ob have given us außer and über. Die Tür iſt unter bem Fenſter = the door is lower, in relation to the window. Cf. the Lat. prepositions *infra, intra, extra, supra, inter*, etc., where the *r* clearly shows a Comparative origin.

142. From leßt, last, comes ber leßtere, the latter;
       „   erſt, first, ber erſtere, the former;
       „   mehr, more, mehrere, several. Cf. Fr. *plusieurs.*

143.   Notes.

Comparison may state

   (*a*) *Equality:*
      Er iſt ebenſo ſtark wie ich. He is as strong as I.

(b) *Superiority*:

Er ift ftärker als id.   He is stronger than I.

(c) *Inferiority*:

Er ift $\begin{Bmatrix} \text{weniger} \\ \text{nidt fo} \end{Bmatrix}$ ftarf als id.   He is not as strong as I.

144. *Measure of Difference* is expressed by um with Acc. or by the simple Acc.:

Er ift (um) einen Kopf größer als id.

He is a head taller than I.

145. *Ratio* is expressed by je..., defto; je..., um fo:

Je mehr er hat, defto mehr verlangt er;

or um fo mehr verlangt er.

The more he has, the more he wants.

146. *Progression* is expressed by immer + Comparative:

Der Kerl wird immer unverfdämter.

The fellow gets more and more insolent.

Er arbeitet immer weniger.   He works less and less.

147. Am + Superlative has two functions:

(a) Adverbial:

Weldher Vogel fingt am füßeften?

Which bird sings most sweetly?

(b) Adjectival:

Er ift am gefährlidften, wenn er fdmeidelt.

He is most dangerous when he flatters.

148. Note the distinction between the adjectival am gefähr= lidften and der gefährlidfte, as in

Er ift von allen meinen Feinden der gefährlidfte.

He is the most dangerous of all my enemies.

Der gefährlichſte compares the Subject with other persons.

Am gefährlichſten compares it with itself in different circumstances.

Cf. Der Sturm war am heftigſten gegen Abend.

The storm was most violent towards evening; i.e. more violent than *it* had been at any other time.

Der Sturm war der heftigſte, den ich je erlebt hatte.

The storm was the most violent that I had ever experienced; i.e. it was more violent than *any other storm* I had known.

149. N.B.

(a) Das iſt $\begin{Bmatrix} \text{höchſt} \\ \text{äußerſt} \end{Bmatrix}$ unangenehm. That is *most* annoying.

(b) Der aller beſte, aller ſtärkſte, uſw.
    The *very* best, strongest, etc.

(c) Er iſt mehr dumm als boshaft.
    He is more stupid than malicious.

(d) Er iſt nichts weniger als dumm.
    He is *anything but* stupid.

(e) Er hat ſich möglichſt viel Mühe gegeben.
    He has taken the greatest possible pains.

(f) Er hat das Möglichſte getan.
    He has done his utmost.

(g) Ich behandle ihn mehr als einen Bruder denn als einen
      Onkel.
    I treat him more as a brother than as an uncle.

Denn is used here to avoid a repetition of als.

THE NUMERALS (das Numeral oder Zahlwort).

150. I. Cardinals (Grundzahlen).

1 Ein, eins	23 dreiundzwanzig
2 zwei	30 dreißig
3 drei	40 vierzig
4 vier	50 fünfzig
5 fünf	60 sechzig
6 sechs	70 siebzig
7 sieben	80 achtzig
8 acht	90 neunzig
9 neun	100 hundert
10 zehn	101 hundertundein(s)
11 elf	102 hundertzwei
12 zwölf	125 hundert fünfundzwanzig
13 dreizehn	200 zweihundert
14 vierzehn	300 dreihundert
15 fünfzehn	1000 tausend
16 sechzehn	2000 zweitausend
17 siebzehn	2500 zweitausend fünfhundert
18 achtzehn	20,000 zwanzigtausend
19 neunzehn	100,000 hunderttausend
20 zwanzig	1,000,000 eine Million
21 einundzwanzig	2,000,000 zwei Millionen
22 zweiundzwanzig	0 Null (fem.)

151. Ein, standing before a noun, is declined like the Indefinite Article:

Er hat nur ein Auge, eine Hand, einen Fuß.

He has only one eye, one hand, one foot.

But when preceded by an adjective of fixed declension it follows the ordinary rule for the declension of adjectives:

In der einen Hand hielt er seinen Hut, in der andern seinen Spazierstock.

In one hand he held his hat, in the other his walking-stick.

Ein, used as a pronoun, is declined like dieſer:

> Einer von meinen Freunden hat's geſehn.
>
> One of my friends (a friend of mine) saw it.
>
> Du haſt ein(e)s vergeſſen. You have forgotten one thing.

In reckoning, the form eins is generally used: eins, zwei— eins, zwei! One, two—one, two! Das Einmaleins, the multi- plication-table.

See also § 210.

152. Zwei and drei, when no declined adjective precedes, must take ⸗er in the Gen. and may take ⸗en in the Dative:

> Aus zwei⸗er Zeugen Munde kommt die Wahrheit.
>
> Out of the mouth of two witnesses cometh truth.

But Die Ausſage dieſer zwei Zeugen iſt wahr.

> The statement of these two witnesses is true.
>
> Niemand kann zwei⸗en Herren (or zwei Herren) dienen.
>
> A man cannot serve two masters.
>
> Er fuhr mit zwei⸗en.   He drove a pair of horses.
>
> Sie kamen zu zwei⸗en.   They came in pairs.

Cf. Er ging auf allen vier⸗en.   He went on all fours.

153. In Compound Numerals the order of the components is as in English, except that the unit comes before the ten: zwei Million(en) zweihundertfünfzigtauſend dreihundert einund⸗ dreißig. 2,250,331.

154. Note that the figures above are, in German, printed 2 250 331, being grouped in threes, and not separated by commas.

155. The comma serves as a decimal point. 10,125 is read zehn, Komma, eins, zwei, fünf.

> 10,50 M. = 10 marks, 50 pfennigs; zehn Mark, fünfzig;
>
> 10,50 m = 10 metres, 50 cm.; zehn Meter, fünfzig.

156. Hunderte, Tausende, Millionen are plural nouns.

Hunderte von Häusern wurden zerstört; Tausende von Menschen kamen um.

Hundreds of houses were destroyed; thousands of men perished.

157. II. **Ordinals** (Ordnungszahlen).

Irregular are 1st. der erste

                 3rd. der dritte

                 8th. der achte.

All the others are formed from the cardinals by adding

to the first nineteen ‑t: der zweite, der vierzehnte;

to the rest ‑st: der vierzigste, der zweiundsechzigste,

                 der hundertste, der tausendste.

158. In Compound Ordinals only the last component takes the ordinal suffix: der hundert und erste, 101st; der zweihundert fünfundzwanzigste, 225th.

    N.B. der letzte, vorletzte, drittletzte; the last, last but one, last but two.

der zweitbeste, second-best.

der erste beste, any one, *le premier venu.*

159. From the Ordinals are formed:

    (a) *Adverbs of Order:* erstens   zweitens   drittens   usw.

                            firstly   secondly   thirdly   etc.

160. (b) *Fractional Numbers:*

das Drittel	third	Hundertstel	hundredth
Viertel	quarter	Tausendstel	thousandth
Fünftel	fifth	Millionstel	millionth.

N.B. die Hälfte, half; eine halbe Stunde, half an hour; ein halbes Pfund, $\frac{1}{2}$ pound; eine Viertelstunde, $\frac{1}{4}$ hour; anderthalb, $1\frac{1}{2}$; dritthalb, $2\frac{1}{2}$; viertehalb, $3\frac{1}{2}$; etc.

161. III. Miscellaneous (Vermischtes).

Multiplicatives:

einfach	single	These are adjectives, and are
doppelt	double	placed between article and noun:
dreifach	threefold	die doppelte Summe, twice the
vierfach	fourfold	amount ;
hundertfach	hundredfold.	das Vierfache, four times as much.

162. *Variatives:*

einerlei, all of one kind   vielerlei, of many kinds
zweierlei, of two kinds   allerlei, of all kinds.

Ich habe zweierlei Tinte.   I have two kinds of ink.
Das ist mir einerlei.   It is all the same to me.

163. *Iteratives:*

einmal, zweimal, dreimal, usw. once, twice, thrice, etc.
Das Einmaleins, the multiplication-table.

164. IV. Date, Time of day, etc. (Datum, Uhr, usw.).

The months		The days of the week
Januar	Juli	Sonntag
Februar	August	Montag
März	September	Dienstag
April	Oktober	Mittwoch
Mai	November	Donnerstag
Juni	Dezember	Freitag
		Samstag or Sonnabend.

165. Der wievielte ist heute?   ⎱ What is the date?
Den wievielten haben wir heute? ⎰

Es ist der 25. (fünfundzwanzigste) November ⎱ It is the 25th
Wir haben den 25. (fünfundzwanzigsten) ⎰· of November.
   November

Am 18. Dezember (Den 18. Dezember) fangen die Ferien an.
The holidays begin on the 18th of December.

At the head of a letter the date is abridged:

den 25. November, or b. 25. November, or b. 25. XI. 27.

It happened *in* 1850.	Es geſchah im Jahre 1850.
In May he sings all day.	Im Mai ſingt er den ganzen Tag.
On Sunday it rained.	Sonntag hat es geregnet.

At the beginning, in the middle, at the end of May.

Anfang, Mitte, Ende Mai.

166.

Vor acht Tagen.	A week ago.
Geſtern vor acht Tagen.	A week ago yesterday.
In acht Tagen.	In a week.
Freitag über acht Tage.	Next Friday week.
Es regnete acht Tage lang.	It rained for a whole week.
Er iſt auf acht Tage verreiſt.	He has gone away for a week.
Er iſt ſeit acht Tagen verreiſt.	He has been away for a week.

167.

Wieviel Uhr iſt es?	What o'clock is it?
Es iſt ein (not eine) Uhr.	It is one o'clock.
Es iſt zehn Minuten nach eins.	It is 10 minutes past one.
Es iſt halb zwei.	It is half past one.
Es iſt viertel nach eins.	It is a quarter past one.
Es iſt zwanzig Minuten vor zwei.	It is 20 minutes to two.
Es iſt viertel vor zwei.	It is a quarter to two.
Punkt zwei (Schlag zwei).	Exactly two, on the stroke of two.
Um zwei Uhr, um halb drei.	At two, at half past two.
Vor ein paar Stunden.	A few hours ago.
Vormittags, nachmittags.	a.m., p.m.

Government of Adjectives.

168. Adjectives may govern a Genitive or Acc., see § 95 and § 96; or a Dative, § 111.

The majority of those adjectives which require a noun to complete their meaning are however followed by a preposition

𝔄n is used after arm, poor; reich, rich.

𝔄uf after achtsam, heedful; aufmerksam, attentive; eiferſüchtig, jealous; neidiſch, envious; ſtolz, proud.

𝔊egen after freundlich, kind; gnädig, gracious.

𝔍n after erfahren, experienced; verliebt, enamoured.

𝔐it after zufrieden, content.

Über after froh, glad; luſtig, merry; traurig, sad.

𝔘m after bekümmert, beſorgt, anxious.

𝔙on after frei, los, ledig. See § 101.

𝔷u after fähig, capable.

𝔅öſe, ärgerlich, angry, take auf of the person and über of the thing.

See under respective prepositions, §§ 415 to 440.

V. PRONOUNS

(das Fürwort oder Pronomen)

PERSONAL PRONOUNS (persönliche Fürwörter).

169.

	1st Person Sing.	2nd Person	3rd Person Masc.	Fem.	Neut.
N.	ich, I	du, thou	er, he	sie, she	es, it
A.	mich	dich	ihn	sie	es
G.	meiner	deiner	seiner	ihrer	—
D.	mir	dir	ihm	ihr	—
	Plur.				
N.	wir	ihr	sie		
A.	uns	euch	sie		
G.	unser	euer	ihrer		
D.	uns	euch	ihnen.		

From these are derived the Possessive Adjectives, § 114, and the Possessive Pronouns, § 180.

With halben, wegen, willen, instead of the Gen. meiner, deiner, usw., a form in -et is used: meinetwegen, meinethalben, um meinet-willen, for my sake.

170. Du is used in the language of religion and poetry, and wherever 'thou' can be used in English. It is also used in addressing relatives, intimate friends, children, animals, and inanimate objects. Officers use it to their men, masters to their menservants, schoolmasters to their boys until they reach the Obersekunda (Fifth Form), after which they are addressed as Sie. All schoolfellows, comrades and messmates use du to each other. This form of address is known as duzen (French *tutoyer*).

The ordinary pronoun of address is the plural of the personal pronoun of the 3rd person, spelt with a capital:

N. & A. Sie; Gen. Ihrer; Dat. Ihnen.

Possessives: Adj., Ihr, Ihre, Ihr; Pronoun, der Ihrige.

171. In old-fashioned German the common form of address
was the plural of the pronoun of the 2nd person, spelt
with a capital: Ihr, Euch, usw. Inferiors were commonly
addressed as Er or Sie; but though Frederick the Great
addressed his ministers of state as Er, this form of
speech would now be regarded even by the humblest as
an insult.

172. Curious concords are the result of the polite use of the
3rd plural:

Seine Majestät haben allergnädigst geruht,...
His Majesty has graciously decreed,...
Eure Hoheit sehen noch schöner aus...
Your Highness looks even handsomer...

173. The genitive and dative of the personal pronouns are
used chiefly of *persons*; when speaking of *things*, use one
of the demonstratives der, dieser, derselbe:

Nachdem er meine Meinung gehört hatte, stimmte er derselben bei.
When he had heard my opinion, he agreed with it.

174. Preposition + Personal Pronoun can be used only of
persons:

Es ist viel Gutes in ihm, ihr, ihnen, usw.
There is much good in him, her, them, etc.

In speaking of things, use compounds of da=, such as:

darin, in it   daraus, out of it   danach, after it
damit, with it   darunter, among them   dahinter, behind it
dafür, for it   dagegen, against it.

Ich bin damit zufrieden.   I am satisfied with it.

When motion is implied, use compounds of hin=:

Wir kamen an ein Gasthaus und traten hinein (or dahinein).
We came to an inn and went into it.

175. **Es.** Note the constructions :

(*a*) Ich bin es; er ist es; sie sind es; sind Sie es? usw.
It is I;   it is he; it is they; is it you?

(*b*) Es ist; es sind; es giebt; es war; usw.
There is, there are, there was, etc.   See § 311.

(*c*) Es *as preparatory subject*:
Es schlug mein Herz; my heart was beating.

(*d*) Es *impersonal*:
Es wurde getanzt; there was dancing.

Hierneben hat es ganz vernehmlich geseufzt und gestöhnt.
There was an audible *sighing* and groaning close by.

(*e*) Er hat es getan;   er hat es mir gesagt.
He did *so*;   he told me *so*.

(*f*) Er ist reich; ich bin es nicht. He is rich; I am not.

REFLEXIVE PRONOUNS (zurückbezügliche Fürwörter).

176. The Personal Pronouns are used as Reflexive and
Reciprocal Pronouns, except for the dative and accusative of the 3rd person, which is sich:

Ich habe mich entschlossen.	I have made up my mind.
Du irrst dich.	You are mistaken.
Setzen wir uns!	Let us sit down.
Sie hat sich Mühe gegeben.	She has taken pains.
Wir haben uns geschlagen.	We have been fighting.
Sie haben sich verziehen.	They have forgiven each other.

177. To avoid confusion between the reflexive and reciprocal
uses, the words selbst, einander, gegenseitig are used:

Sie haben sich selbst verziehen.
They have forgiven *themselves*.

Sie haben einander geholfen   } They have helped each
Sie haben sich gegenseitig geholfen}   other.

178. Selbst or selber may also be used to emphasise a nominative:

Das habe ich selbst gesehen.   I saw it myself.

Der König selbst⎫
Selbst der König⎭ hat kein besseres Pferd.

The King himself (even the King) has not a better horse.

179. Sich must be used for the 3rd person after a preposition,
when referring to the subject of the sentence:

Er hatte kein Geld bei sich.   He had no money on him.

Haben Sie nichts für sich (or sich selbst) gekauft?

Have you bought nothing for yourself?

POSSESSIVE PRONOUNS (possessive Fürwörter).

180. There are three forms:

(a) der meinige, die meinige, das meinige; mine.
    der deinige, seinige, ihrige, unsrige, eurige, ihrige.

(b) der meine, die meine, das meine; mine.
    der deine, seine, ihre, unsre, eure, ihre.

(c) meiner, meine, mein(e)s; mine.
    deiner, seiner, ihrer, unsrer, eurer, ihrer.

181. Der meinige, der meine, and all the other forms in (a) and
(b) are declined as Definite Article + Adjective; meiner,
deiner, etc. are declined like dieser:

Mein Fuß ist länger als deiner, or der deinige, or der deine.
My foot is longer than yours.

Unsre Freunde haben Ihre (die Ihrigen, die Ihren) besucht.
Our friends have called on yours.

Mein, dein, etc. are sometimes used predicatively, without
inflexion:

Der Hut ist mein.   That hat is mine.

Die Feder ist mein.   The pen is mine.

(More commonly: der Hut gehört mir.)

182. Note:

Das Mein und Dein.	Meum et tuum.
Die Meinigen.	My people.
Grüße an die Deinigen!	Kind regards to your people.
Gib jedem das Seine.	Give every man his due.
Er hat das Seinige getan.	He has done his best.

DEMONSTRATIVE PRONOUNS (demonstrative Fürwörter).

183. The most important are

der, die, das, ⎫ that.   dieser, diese, dieses, this.
jener, jene, jenes, ⎭   solcher, solche, solches, such.
derjenige, diejenige, dasjenige, that (French *celui*).
derselbe, dieselbe, dasselbe, the same.
derlei,
dergleichen, ⎬ (indeclinable) such.
solcherlei,

184. Dieser, jener, solcher, are declined like the corresponding adjectives, §§ 112, 113; derjenige and derselbe are declined as der + Adjective; see § 122.

Der is declined:
                             Pl.

N.	der	die	das	die
A.	den	die	das	die
G.	dessen	deren	dessen	deren or derer
D.	dem	der	dem	denen.

Note. The demonstrative being always stressed, the stem e is always long and narrow, except in dessen. Der = deːr, den = deːn, dem = deːm.

The gen. pl. derer is used only as the antecedent of a relative:

Er fragte nach den Namen derer, die tapfer gefochten hatten.

He enquired the names of those who had fought bravely.
But, Es gibt deren wenige, there are few of them.

185. Dergleichen, derlei, ſolcherlei may be used adjectivally or pronominally:

Dergleichen Leute mag ich nicht gern leiden.

I don't like people of that sort.

Ich habe nichts dergleichen geſehen.

I have never seen anything of the kind.

Danton, Robespierre und dergleichen, ...et hoc genus omne.

Notes on the Use of the Demonstrative Pronouns.

186. Der, dieſer, derſelbe are often used instead of personal pronouns, especially to avoid possible confusion:

Ich habe einen Brief von ihm erhalten und denſelben ungeleſen verbrannt.

I had a letter from him and burned *it* unread.

Er ſah ſeinen Freund und deſſen Frau.

He saw his friend and his (the latter's) wife.

Dieſer and jener are used, like the French *celui-ci, celui-là*, for 'the latter', 'the former':

Ich habe Hans und Grete eingeladen; dieſe kommt, jener aber hat ſich entſchuldigt.

I have invited H. and G.; she is coming, but he has refused.

187. Dies and das are invariable before ſein + noun:

Das iſt meine Mutter, das ſind meine Schweſtern.

That is my mother, those are my sisters.

But Sind Sie der Herr? — Der bin ich ja.

Are you the master? — I am. (*Noun preceding.*)

188. Der, des, dem, combine with some prepositions and nouns:

deswegen,⎫ on that account
deshalb, ⎭

dergeſtalt, in such a way

dermaßen, to such a degree

trotzdem, in spite of that

deſſenungeachtet, notwithstanding.

189. Instead of Preposition + Demonstrative, the adverbs darin, dadurch, damit, hierin, hierdurch, hiermit, etc. are used. The stress accent in these cases falls on the *first* syllable.

RELATIVE PRONOUNS (relative ober bezügliche Fürwörter).

190. 1. Welcher, welche, welches; declined like biefer.

    2. Der.

	M.	F.	N.	Pl.
N.	ber	bie	bas	bie
A.	ben	bie	bas	bie
G.	beffen	beren	beffen	beren
D.	bem	ber	bem	benen.

191. Welcher is used as a relative pronoun in all cases *except the genitive*:

    Er ist ber einzige, welcher (or ber) Ihnen helfen kann.
    He is the only man who can help you.

    Hier ist ber Mann, beffen (not welches) Rat Sie begehren.
    Here is the man whose advice you desire.

192. Der is generally preferred to welcher, and *must* be used when the antecedent is a personal pronoun or a vocative:

    Auch er kann es nicht, ber (not welcher) boch fast alles kann.
    Even he cannot do it, and he can do almost anything.

    Das wiffen wir, bie wir bie Gemfen jagen.
    We who hunt the chamois know that well.

    Der bu von bem Himmel bist, ... füßer Friebe!
    Sweet Peace, that comest from Heaven.

Note in these last two examples the repetition of the personal pronoun after the relative, the latter being in the nominative case. An alternative construction is to put all verbs and pronouns in the relative clause into the third person:

    Dürft Ihr von Liebe reben unb von Treue,
    Der treulos wirb an feinen nächsten Pflichten?
    What right have you to speak of love and loyalty,
    You who are disloyal to your nearest duty?

See §§ 567 to 570.

INTERROGATIVE PRONOUNS (fragende Fürwörter).

193. Wer? Was?

    N. Wer? Who?   Was? What?
    A. Wen?   Was?
    G. Wessen?   (Wes?)
    D. Wem?   —

194. Wer is used of persons without distinction of sex; was of things:

    Wer ist Frau Schulze? Who is Frau Schulze?

(Wie ist Frau Schulze? means: What sort of person is Frau S.?)

195. Wie is used in certain expressions as a politer substitute for was:

    Wie ist Ihr werter Name?⎫
    Wie heißen Sie?   ⎬ What is your name?
                  ⎭
    Wie beliebt? I beg your pardon. (What did you say?)

196. Wer and was have no plural. The singular form may have a plural meaning:

Wer war alles zugegen? What people were there?
Ich weiß nicht, wer sie waren. I don't know who they were.
Was du alles weißt! What hosts of things you know!

197. Was, strictly speaking, is not used after prepositions, interrogative adverbs being used instead, such as worin? in what? woraus? out of what? weshalb? weswegen? why? womit? with what? Compare darin, daraus, etc.

    Wozu ist Geld gut? What is money good for?

198. Wer and was are often used for Demonstrative + Relative, and are preferable to the clumsy derjenige, welcher:

    Wer mit dem Leben spielt, kommt nie zurecht.
    He who plays with life will never prosper.
    Was du sagst, ist wahr. What you say is true.

    Cf. Wen der Herr liebt, den züchtigt Er.
    Whom the Lord loveth, He chasteneth.

199. Was is used as a Relative when the antecedent is

(*a*) A Neuter Pronoun or Pronominal Adjective; e.g. das, alles, viel(es), nichts, etwas, etc.:

> Alles, was du kochst, ist gut.
>
> Everything you cook is good.

(*b*) Das + a Neuter Adjective in the Superlative:

> Das Beste, was du wissen kannst, ...
>
> The best thing you can know, ...

(*c*) A clause:

> Er war unverschämt, was mich sehr ärgerte.
>
> He was insolent, which made me very angry.

200. A similar use is made of wo and its compounds wodurch, wovon, womit, worin, etc.:

> Er hat zu viel gegessen, wodurch er krank geworden ist.
>
> He has eaten too much, from which cause he has fallen sick.
>
> Das ist etwas, wovon ich nichts weiß.
>
> That is a matter of which I know nothing.

These forms are also used, less correctly, in reference to nouns:

> Der Bleistift, womit ich schreibe.
>
> The pencil with which I write.

This construction, though commonly used in conversation, should not be imitated; say rather,

> der Bleistift, mit dem ich schreibe.

Wo however, being a relative, may be freely used:

> Die Stadt, wo wir wohnen....   The town we live in....

201. Welcher, welche, welches, is really an adjective, but can also be used pronominally with reference to a noun:

> Welches Buch lesen Sie? Which book are you reading?
>
> Welches von Ihren Büchern haben Sie verloren?
>
> Which of your books have you lost?

202. Welch, in exclamations, is uninflected when followed by the indefinite article or an adjective :

> Welch ein Mann! What a man!
> Welch gräßliches Ereignis! What a dreadful deed!
> O welch ein edler Geist ist hier zerstört!
> O what a noble mind is here o'erthrown!

203. Wer, was, welcher, and other interrogative words, e.g. wie, wo, are often used as indefinites :

> Haft du was gesehen?
> Have you seen anything?

204.

    (*a*) Was für ein? was für eine? was für ein? }   What

    (*b*) Was für einer? was für eine? was für ein(e)s? } kind of...?

The first is adjectival, the second pronominal.

The was für is invariable, only the ein, einer, etc. being declined :

Adj. Was für ein Fisch ist das? What kind of fish is that?
      Was für einen Fisch hast du gefangen?
      What kind of fish did you catch?
      In was für einem Hause wohnt er?
      What kind of house does he live in?
      Was für Fische sind das? What kind of fish are those?

Pron. Ich habe ein Motorrad gekauft.—Was für eins?
      I have bought a motor bicycle.—What kind?
      Der Herr da ist Schriftsteller.—Was für einer?
      That gentleman is a writer?—What sort of writer?
      Wir haben zwei Fische gefangen.—Was für welche? or Was für?
      We have caught two fishes.—What kind?
      Wir haben Wein im Keller —Was für Wein? or Was für
                             welchen? or Was für?
      We have wine in the cellar.—What sort (of wine)?

MISCELLANEOUS PRONOUNS AND ADJECTIVES.

205. All.

Wir alle.	All of us.
Alle Schüler.	All the boys.
All mein Geld.	All my money.
All diese Häuser.	All these houses.
Alles stieg aus.	Everybody got out.
Die Butter ist alle.	The butter is finished.
Alle Tage.	Every day.
Er läßt sich alles gefallen.	He will stand *any*thing.
But den ganzen Tag.	All day.
Ganz Europa.	All Europe.

206. Ander.

Den andern Tag.	Next day.
Vor ein paar Tagen.	The other day.
Anders.	Otherwise, differently.
Ich kann nicht anders.	I cannot help it.
Wer anders? Jemand anders.	Who else? Someone else.
Etwas anders; von etwas anderm.	Something else; of something else.
Anderthalb.	One and a half.

207. Beid-.

Beides hat recht.	We (you, they) are both right.
Wir sind alle beide krank.	We are both ill.
Einer (keiner) von beiden.	One or the other; neither.
Zwischen den beiden Linien.	Between the two lines.

N.B. *Both you and your brother.* Sowohl Sie als Ihr Bruder.

208. Eigen.

Ein eignes Haus.	A house of my own (your own, etc.).
Ein Leibeigner.	A bondman, serf.

209. Einander (indeclinable), *each other.*

Sie haben einander geholfen.	They have helped each other.
Sie sind auseinander gekommen.	They have parted.
Drei Tage hintereinander.	Three days in succession.
Zehn Zentimeter voneinander.	Four inches apart.
Durcheinander.	In confusion.

210. Einer (pronoun). See §§ 151, 217.

Ich habe zwei Jungen gefunden; hier ist einer.	I have found two boys; here is one.
So etwas kann einen sehr ärgern.	That sort of thing can make one very angry.
Einer von meinen Freunden.	A friend of mine.
Haben Sie so einen, ꞏe, ꞏes?	Have you one like this?
Einer von beiden; (keiner v. b.).	One of the two; neither.
N.B. *The one that you have lost.*	Derjenige, den Sie verloren haben.

211. Ein paar (indecl.), *a few*; **ein Paar**, *a pair.*

Nach ein paar Tagen.	A few days after.
Mit einem Paar Handschuhen.	With a pair of gloves.

212. Etwas.

Ich habe etwas zu sagen.	I have *some*thing to say.
Wenn ich etwas zu sagen hätte.	If I had *any*thing to say.
Etwas schönes.	Something fine.
Haben Sie so etwas?	Have you anything like this?
Geben Sie mir was (= etwas).	Give me something.
Er ist etwas dumm.	He is rather stupid.
N.B. Hast du etwa Geld bei dir?	Do you happen to have any money on you?

213. Jeder.

Er kann jeden Augenblick ankommen.	He may arrive at any moment.
Das kann ein jeder.	Any one can do that.
N.B. *He gave them 2 marks each.*	Er gab ihnen je 2 Mark.

214. Irgenð ein, irgenð einer, etc. *Affirmatively,* some (one) or other. *In a Question or Condition,* any (one) at all.

Aus irgenð einem Grunde. For some reason or other.

Er hat dir irgenð etwas gesagt.
He has said something to you.

Ist irgenð eine Hoffnung vorhanden?
Is there any hope at all?

Compare: Was ich irgenð kann....
Anything I can possibly do.

215. Jeðermann: Gen. jeðermanns, D. and A. jeðermann.

Er ist jeðermanns Freund. He is everybody's friend.

216. Jemand: Gen. jemands, D. and A. jemand.

Es kommt jemand. There is somebody coming.
Wenn jemand kommt. If anybody comes.

217. Man, weakened form of Mann (cf. French *on*, from Latin *homo*).

Man is used only in the Nom. The other cases are taken from einer (§ 210). The reflexive is sich, the possessive sein.

Man glaubt. It is believed.
Man muß sich in Acht nehmen. One has to be careful.
Man nehme sich in Acht. Please be careful.

218. Manch (undeclined), **mancher, -e, -es.**

Manch ein Mann. Many a man.
Manch edler Ritter. Many a noble knight.
Mancher Mann. Mancher eðle Ritter.
Mancher fürchtet sich vor Gespenstern.
Many a man is afraid of ghosts.
Ich habe so manches zu schaffen. I have much to do.

219. Nichts: D. and A. nichts; no Gen.

> Nichts gutes; zu nichts gutem.
> Nothing good; for no good purpose.
> Nichts als...; faſt nichts.
> Nothing but...; hardly anything.
> Nichts anders; ſonſt nichts. Nothing else.
> Nichts weniger als.... Anything but.
> Er iſt nichts weniger als fleißig.
> He is *anything but* industrious.

220. Niemand: D. and A. niemand, Gen. niemands.

> Niemand anders; ſonſt niemand. No one else.
> Niemand als...; faſt niemand.
> None but...; hardly anybody.

221. Solch (undeclined), **ſolcher, -e, -es.** See § 112.

Solch ein Mann, or ein ſolcher Mann. Such a man.

Solch ein großes Haus; ein ſo großes Haus; or, colloquially,
ſo ein großes Haus. Such a great house.

Solch große Häuſer. Such great houses.

Solche, die nicht arbeiten. Such as (those who) do not work.

Other German equivalents of the English 'such':

Ein geſcheiter Kerl, wie Sie. Such a smart fellow as you.

Manche Leute, wie z. B. Schmitt. Many people, such as Schmitt.

Hier iſt, ſagt' er, ein Mädchen, ſo wie ihr im Hauſe ſie wünſchet.
Here, said he, is just such a maid as you desire in the house.

Das war ein Kampf, wie ihn noch keiner geſehen hat.
That was such a battle as no man ever yet beheld.

Ein Gewitter, wie ich noch keines erlebt hatte.
A storm such as I had never before experienced.

See also § 569, and compare the French: C'étaient des gens
comme je n'en avais jamais vu.

VI. VERBS
(das Verbum, das Zeitwort)

GENERAL REMARKS ON THE CONJUGATIONS
(die Konjugation).

222. As in English, there are two Conjugations, the Strong and the Weak.

223. The Principal Parts of a Verb are (1) the Present Infinitive, (2) the Past (Imperfect) Indicative, and (3) the Past Participle.

224. The Infinitive adds *en or *n to the stem: fag*en, say; reb*en, speak.

225. **Weak Verbs** form the Past by adding *te or *ete to the stem, and the Past Participle by prefixing the augment ge* and adding *t or *et:

fag*en,	say,	fag*te,	ge*fag*t.
reb*en,	speak,	reb*ete,	ge*reb*et.

226. **Strong Verbs** form the Past by a simple change of vowel, called *Ablaut*; the Past Participle prefixes the augment and adds the suffix *en, with or without *Ablaut*:

brech*en,	break,	brach,	ge*broch*en.
fall*en,	fall,	fiel,	ge*fall*en.

227. **The Augment** occurs only before a stressed syllable. It is therefore not found in the Past Participles of (*a*) verbs with an unstressed prefix, e.g. zerbrechen, P.P. zerbrochen; verfallen, P.P. verfallen; (*b*) verbs with the suffix *ieren, e.g. ftubieren, P.P. ftubiert; oxybieren, P.P. oxybiert; (*c*) offenbáren, miaúen, krakeélen, pofaúnen.

228. There are only two simple tenses, the Present and the Past. The others are formed with the auxiliaries (Hilfszeitwörter) fein, haben and werden. Sein and haben are used to form the Perfect, Pluperfect, Future-Perfect and Conditional Perfect. Bleiben, ſein, and most intransitive verbs indicating change of place or state take ſein, e.g. kommen, gehen, fallen, laufen, ſterben, wachſen; the rest take haben.

Die Sonne iſt aufgegangen; die Nebel ſind verſchwunden.
The sun has risen; the mists have vanished.

Hier hat der Baum geſtanden; ich habe ihn oft geſehen.
The tree stood here: I often saw it.

229. Werden is used with the Infinitive to form the Future and Conditional, and with the Past Participle to form the Passive Voice:

Ich werde um zwei Uhr ankommen.
I shall arrive at two o'clock.

Ihr würdet nicht anders gehandelt haben, als ich.
You would have acted just as I did.

Der Kaufmann wurde von Räubern überfallen.
The merchant was attacked by robbers.

230. In addition to these three auxiliaries, there are six others, known as Modal Auxiliaries, or Auxiliaries of Mood. They are dürfen, können, mögen, müſſen, ſollen, wollen. See § 288.

231. THE AUXILIARY VERB **Sein**, TO BE.
Principal Parts: ſein, war, geweſen.

Indicative.	Subjunctive.
PRESENT.	
ich bin	ich ſei
du biſt	du ſeieſt
er iſt	er ſei
wir ſind	wir ſeien
ihr ſeid	ihr ſeiet
ſie ſind.	ſie ſeien.

Indicative.	Subjunctive.

PAST.

ich war	ich wäre
du warst	du wärest
er war	er wäre
wir waren	wir wären
ihr war(e)t	ihr wäret
ſie waren.	ſie wären.

PERFECT.

ich bin geweſen	ich ſei geweſen
du biſt geweſen	du ſeieſt geweſen
er iſt geweſen	er ſei geweſen
wir ſind geweſen	wir ſeien geweſen
ihr ſeid geweſen	ihr ſeiet geweſen
ſie ſind geweſen.	ſie ſeien geweſen.

PLUPERFECT.

ich war geweſen	ich wäre geweſen
du warſt geweſen	du wäreſt geweſen
er war geweſen	er wäre geweſen
wir waren geweſen	wir wären geweſen
ihr war(e)t geweſen	ihr wäret geweſen
ſie waren geweſen.	ſie wären geweſen.

FUTURE-PERFECT.

ich werde geweſen ſein	ich werde geweſen ſein
du wirſt geweſen ſein	du werdeſt geweſen ſein
er wird geweſen ſein	er werde geweſen ſein
wir werden geweſen ſein	wir werden geweſen ſein
ihr werdet geweſen ſein	ihr werdet geweſen ſein
ſie werden geweſen ſein.	ſie werden geweſen ſein.

Indicative.	Subjunctive.

FUTURE.

ich werde sein	ich werde sein
du wirst sein	du werdest sein
er wird sein	er werde sein
wir werden sein	wir werden sein
ihr werdet sein	ihr werdet sein
sie werden sein.	sie werden sein.

Conditional (Future in the Past Subjunctive).	Conditional-Perfect (Future-Perfect in the Past Subjunctive).
ich würde sein	ich würde gewesen sein
du würdest sein	du würdest gewesen sein
er würde sein	er würde gewesen sein
wir würden sein	wir würden gewesen sein
ihr würdet sein	ihr würdet gewesen sein
sie würden sein.	sie würden gewesen sein.

Imperative.

Sing. —   *Plur.* ⎰ Seien wir! Laßt uns sein!
⎱ Wollen wir sein! Wir wollen sein!

Sei!	Seid! (polite form, Seien Sie!)
Er sei!	Sie seien! Sie sollen sein!

Note. The only really imperative forms are the 2nd pers. sing. and 2nd pers. plur. The other persons are borrowed from the Subj. or formed by means of auxiliary verbs. See § 323.

Infinitive.

PRESENT. sein.   *PERFECT.* gewesen sein.

Participles.

PRESENT. seiend.   *PAST.* gewesen.

232. THE AUXILIARY VERB Werden, *TO BECOME.*

Principal Parts: werben, wurbe, geworben.

Indicative.	Subjunctive.

PRESENT.

ich werbe	ich werbe
bu wirst	bu werbest
er wirb	er werbe
wir werben	wir werben
ihr werbet	ihr werbet
sie werben.	sie werben.

PAST.

ich wurbe	ich würbe
bu wurbest	bu würbest
er wurbe	er würbe
wir wurben	wir würben
ihr wurbet	ihr würbet
sie wurben.	sie würben.

PERFECT.

ich bin geworben	ich sei geworben
bu bist geworben	bu seiest geworben
er ist geworben	er sei geworben
wir sinb geworben	wir seien geworben
ihr seib geworben	ihr seiet geworben
sie sinb geworben.	sie seien geworben.

PLUPERFECT.

ich war geworben, etc.	ich wäre geworben, etc.

FUTURE-PERFECT.

ich werbe geworben sein, etc.	ich werbe geworben sein, etc.

FUTURE.

ich werbe sein, etc.	ich werbe sein, etc.

Conditional.	Conditional Perfect.
idy würde werben, etc.	idy würde geworden ſein, etc.

Imperative.

Sing. — *Plur.* Werben wir! Laßt uns
werben! etc.

Werbe! Werbet!
Er werbe! Sie werben! Sie ſollen
werben!

Infinitive.

PRESENT. werben. PERFECT. geworden ſein.

Participles.

PRESENT. werbenb. PAST. geworden.

233. THE AUXILIARY VERB **Haben**, *TO HAVE.*
Principal Parts: haben, hatte, gehabt.

Indicative.	Subjunctive.

PRESENT.

idy habe	idy habe
bu haſt	bu habeſt
er hat	er habe
wir haben	wir haben
ihr habt	ihr habet
ſie haben.	ſie haben.

PAST.

idy hatte	idy hätte
bu hatteſt	bu hätteſt
er hatte	er hätte
wir hatten	wir hätten
ihr hattet	ihr hättet
ſie hatten.	ſie hätten.

Verbs

Indicative.	Subjunctive.

PERFECT.

ich habe gehabt	ich habe gehabt
du haft gehabt	du habeft gehabt
er hat gehabt	er habe gehabt
wir haben gehabt	wir haben gehabt
ihr habt gehabt	ihr habet gehabt
fie haben gehabt.	fie haben gehabt.

PLUPERFECT.

ich hatte gehabt	ich hätte gehabt
du hatteft gehabt	du hätteft gehabt
er hatte gehabt	er hätte gehabt
wir hatten gehabt	wir hätten gehabt
ihr hattet gehabt	ihr hättet gehabt
fie hatten gehabt.	fie hätten gehabt.

FUTURE-PERFECT.

ich werde gehabt haben, etc.	ich werde gehabt haben, etc.

FUTURE.

ich werde haben, etc.	ich werde haben, etc.

Conditional.	Conditional Perfect.
ich würde haben, etc.	ich würde gehabt haben, etc.

Imperative.

Sing. Habe!	*Plur.* Habt!

Infinitive.

PRESENT. haben.	PERFECT. gehabt haben.

Participles.

PRESENT. habend.	PAST. gehabt.

234. THE WEAK VERB **Sagen,** *TO SAY.*

Principal Parts: ſagen, ſagte, geſagt.

Indicative.	Subjunctive.

PRESENT.

ich ſage	ich ſage
du ſagſt	du ſageſt
er ſagt	er ſage
wir ſagen	wir ſagen
ihr ſagt	ihr ſaget
ſie ſagen.	ſie ſagen.

PAST.

ich ſagte	ich ſagte
du ſagteſt	du ſagteſt
er ſagte	er ſagte
wir ſagten	wir ſagten
ihr ſagtet	ihr ſagtet
ſie ſagten.	ſie ſagten.

PERFECT.

ich habe geſagt, etc.	ich habe geſagt, etc.

PLUPERFECT.

ich hatte geſagt, etc.	ich hätte geſagt, etc.

FUTURE-PERFECT.

ich werde geſagt haben, etc.	ich werde geſagt haben, etc.

FUTURE.

ich werde ſagen, etc.	ich werde ſagen, etc.

Conditional.	Conditional Perfect.
ich würde ſagen, etc.	ich würde geſagt haben, etc.

Imperative.

Sing. Sage!   *Plur.* Sagt!

Infinitive.

PRESENT. sagen.   PERFECT. gesagt haben.

Participles.

PRESENT. sagend.   PAST. gesagt.

NOTES ON THE WEAK CONJUGATION (schwache Konjugation).

235. Verbs in ⸗eln drop the e of the stem before the termination ⸗e: tabeln, to blame, ich tab⸗le; they also drop the ⸗e of the termination before ⸗n: wir tab⸗eln, tab⸗elnd.

236. Verbs in ⸗ern may drop the e of the stem before the termination ⸗e: ich wand⸗ere or wand⸗re.

   They must drop the ⸗e of the termination before ⸗n; wir wandern, wandernd.

237. Stems ending in ⸗b or ⸗t are always followed by e; e.g. enden (to end); du end⸗eft, er end⸗et, end⸗ete, geend⸗et. This applies also to strong verbs.

   The same applies to stems ending in ⸗m or ⸗n preceded by any consonant except l and r; e.g. atmen (to breathe), du atm⸗eft, atm⸗ete, geatm⸗et; zeichnen (to draw), du zeichn⸗eft, zeichn⸗ete, gezeichn⸗et. But lernen (to learn), du lern⸗ft, lern⸗te, gelern⸗t.

238. Stems ending in a sibilant, s, ff, ß, z, sch, add ⸗e before ⸗ft; e.g. grüßen (to greet), du grüß⸗eft; fassen (to seize), du fass⸗eft; überraschen (to surprise), du überrasch⸗eft; setzen (to set), setz⸗eft.

   The 2nd pers. sing. pres. ind. of such verbs often contracts: du setzeft or setzt; grüßeft or grüßt; fasseft or faßt.

   This applies also to strong verbs: du läffeft, läßt; miffeft, mißt.

   N.B. ch is not a sibilant. Lachen (to laugh), du lachft.

239. THE STRONG VERB 𝔗𝔯𝔞𝔤𝔢𝔫, *TO CARRY.*

Principal Parts: tragen, trug, getragen.

Indicative.	Subjunctive.

PRESENT.

ich trage	ich trage
du trägst	du tragest
er trägt	er trage
wir tragen	wir tragen
ihr tragt	ihr traget
sie tragen.	sie tragen.

PAST.

ich trug	ich trüge
du trugst	du trügest
er trug	er trüge
wir trugen	wir trügen
ihr trugt	ihr trüget
sie trugen.	sie trügen.

PERFECT.

ich habe getragen, etc.	ich habe getragen, etc.

PLUPERFECT.

ich hatte getragen, etc.	ich hätte getragen, etc.

FUTURE-PERFECT.

ich werde getragen haben, etc.	ich werde getragen haben, etc.

FUTURE.

ich werde tragen, etc.	ich werde tragen, etc.

Conditional.	Conditional Perfect.
ich würde tragen, etc.	ich würde getragen haben, etc.

6-2

Imperative.

Sing. Trage!　　　　　　　　*Plur.* Tragt!

Infinitive.

PRESENT. tragen.　　　　　PERFECT. getragen haben.

Participles.

PRESENT. tragend.　　　　PAST. getragen.

NOTES ON THE STRONG CONJUGATION (starke Konjugation).

240. The Verbs of this Conjugation are grouped according to the stem-vowel and its Ablaut.

241. In the Pres. Ind. most strong verbs modify the vowel in the 2nd and 3rd sing., e.g. ich trage, du trägst, er trägt; those with e-stems change short e into i and long e into ie, and show the same change of vowel in the Imperative sing., e.g. ich spreche (I speak), du sprichst, er spricht; sprich!

ich befehle (I order), du befiehlst, er befiehlt; befiehl!

In the Imperative, verbs which modify do not add *e*; with others the termination is optional, but is usually omitted in conversation.

242. The Past Subj. is formed by modifying (if modifiable) the vowel of the Past Ind. and adding *e*: tragen, trug, ich trüge; sprechen, sprach, ich spräche.

With vowel not modifiable:

reißen (tear), riß, ich risse; reiben (rub), rieb, ich riebe.

Where a verb has alternative forms for the Past Subj., e.g. werfen (throw), warf, ich wärfe or würfe, the one which is pronounced less like the Present is to be preferred. The only reason for its survival is the natural desire to distinguish between these tenses. This applies to those verbs of Group C, below, which have a short vowel in the past tense.

List of Strong Verbs Arranged by Groups.

Verbs with *s* prefixed are conjugated with ſein.

243. Group A. Ablaut: a—u—a.

Infinitive		Past	Past Participle	3rd sing. Pres. Ind.	Imperative	Past Subj.
Baden	bake	buf	gebaden	bädt	bade	büfe
s Fahren	drive	fuhr	gefahren	fährt	fahre	führe
Graben	dig	grub	gegraben	gräbt	grabe	grübe
Laben	load	lub	gelaben	lädt	labe	lübe
Schaffen	create	schuf	geschaffen	schafft	schaffe	schüfe
Schlagen	strike	schlug	geschlagen	schlägt	schlage	schlüge
Tragen	carry	trug	getragen	trägt	trage	trüge
s Wachsen	grow	wuchs	gewachsen	wächst	wachse	wüchse
Waschen	wash	wusch	gewaschen	wäscht	wasche	wüsche

244. Group B. Ablaut: a—ie—a.

Infinitive		Past	Past Participle	3rd sing. Pres. Ind.	Imperative	Past Subj.
Blaſen	blow	blies	geblaſen	bläſt	blaſe	blieſe
Braten	roast	briet	gebraten	brät	brate	briete
s Fallen	fall	fiel	gefallen	fällt	falle	fiele
Gefallen	please	gefiel	gefallen	gefällt	gefalle	gefiele
Halten	hold	hielt	gehalten	hält	halt(e)	hielte
Laſſen	let	ließ	gelaſſen	läßt	laſſ(e)	ließe
Raten	advise	riet	geraten	rät	rate	riete
Schlafen	sleep	schlief	geschlafen	schläft	schlafe	schliefe

Also:

Infinitive		Past	Past Participle	3rd sing. Pres. Ind.	Imperative	Past Subj.
Fangen	catch	fing	gefangen	fängt	fang(e)	finge
{ Gangen / Hängen }	hang	hing	gehangen	hängt	hange	hinge
Hauen	hew	hieb	gehauen	haut	haue	hiebe
Heißen	call	hieß	geheißen	heißt	heiß(e)	hieße

Infinitive		Past	Past Participle	3rd sing. Pres. Ind.	Imperative	Past Subj.
s Laufen	run	lief	gelaufen	läuft	lauf(e)	liefe
Rufen	call	rief	gerufen	ruft	rufe	riefe
Stoßen	thrust	stieß	gestoßen	stößt	stoß(e)	stieße

245. Group C. (i) Bergen   Ablaut: ĕ—ă (ā)—ŏ.

Infinitive		Past	Past Participle	3rd sing. Pres. Ind.	Imperative	Past Subj.
Bergen	hide	barg	geborgen	birgt	birg	bärge
Bersten	burst	barst	geborsten	birst	berste or birst	bärste or börste
Brechen	break	brāch	gebrochen	bricht	brich	bräche
Dreschen	thrash	{ brāsch / brōsch	gedroschen	drischt	drisch	{ bräsche / brösche
Erschrecken	be frightened	erschrāk	erschrocken	erschrickt	erschrick	erschräke
Gelten	be worth	galt	gegolten	gilt	gilt	gälte or gölte
Helfen	help	half	geholfen	hilft	hilf	hälfe or hülfe
Schelten	scold	schalt	gescholten	schilt	schilt	schälte or schölte
Sprechen	speak	sprāch	gesprochen	spricht	sprich	spräche
Stechen	sting	stāch	gestochen	sticht	stich	stäche
s Stecken	stick (intrans.)	stāk (steckte)	gesteckt	steckt	stecke	stäke or steckte
Sterben	die	starb	gestorben	stirbt	stirb	stürbe
Treffen	hit	trāf	getroffen	trifft	triff	träfe
Verderben	spoil	verdarb	verdorben	verdirbt	verdirb	verdürbe
Werben	sue	warb	geworben	wirbt	wirb	würbe
s Werden	become	ward (wurde)	geworden	wird	werde	würde
Werfen	throw	warf	geworfen	wirft	wirf	würfe or wörfe

Also:

Infinitive		Past	Past Participle	3rd sing. Pres. Ind.	Imperative	Past Subj.
Kommen	come	kām	gekommen	kommt	komm(e)	käme

246. Ablaut: ĭ—ă—ŏ.

Infinitive		Past	Past Participle	3rd sing. Pres. Ind.	Imperative	Past Subj.
(ii) Beginnen	begin	begann	begonnen	beginnt	beginne	begänne or begönne
Gewinnen	win	gewann	gewonnen	gewinnt	gewinne	gewänne or gewönne
s Rinnen	run	rann	geronnen	rinnt	rinn(e)	ränne or rönne

Infinitive	Meaning	Imperative	Present (3rd sg.)	Past	Past Participle	Past Subjunctive
s Schwimmen	swim	schwimme	schwimmt	schwamm	geschwommen	schwämme or schwömme
Sinnen	think	sinne	sinnt	sann	gesonnen	sänne or sönne
Spinnen	spin	spinne	spinnt	spann	gesponnen	spänne or spönne

247. Ablaut: ē (ā)—ā—ō.

(iii)

Infinitive	Meaning	Imperative	Present (3rd sg.)	Past	Past Participle	Past Subjunctive
Befehlen	command	befiehl	befiehlt	befahl	befohlen	beföhle or befähle
Empfehlen	recommend	empfiehl	empfiehlt	empfahl	empfohlen	empföhle or empfähle
Gebären	bear	gebier	gebärt / gebiert	gebar	geboren	gebäre
Nehmen	take	nimm	nimmt	nahm	genommen	nähme
Stehlen	steal	stiehl	stiehlt	stahl	gestohlen	stöhle or stähle

248. Group D. Ablaut: ī—ā—ŭ. All these verbs are conjugated exactly like binden.

Infinitive	Meaning	Imperative	Present (3rd sg.)	Past	Past Participle	Past Subjunctive
Binden	bind	binde	bindet	band	gebunden	bände
Dingen	hire			dang	gedungen	
Dringen	press			drang	gedrungen	
Finden	find			fand	gefunden	
s Gelingen	succeed			gelang	gelungen (third person only)	
Klingen	sound			klang	geklungen	
Ringen	wring			rang	gerungen	
Schlingen	sling			schlang	geschlungen	
s Schwinden	vanish			schwand	geschwunden (usually in compound verschwinden)	
Schwingen	swing			schwang	geschwungen	
Singen	sing			sang	gesungen	
s Sinken	sink			sank	gesunken	
Springen	spring			sprang	gesprungen	
Stinken	stink			stank	gestunken	
Trinken	drink			trank	getrunken	
Winden	wind			wand	gewunden	
Zwingen	force			zwang	gezwungen	

Also:

Infinitive	Meaning	Imperative	Present (3rd sg.)	Past	Past Participle	Past Subjunctive
Schinden	flay	schinde	schindet	schund	geschunden	schünde

249. Group E. Ablaut: ie (ĕ, ĭ, ă, au, ö)—ŏ—ŏ.

Infinitive	die out	Past	Past Participle	3rd sing. Pres. Ind.	Imperative	Past Subj.
(i) s Erlöſchen	die out	erloſch	erloſchen	erliſcht	erliſch	erlöſche
Fechten	fight	focht	gefochten	ficht	ficht	föchte
Flechten	plait	flocht	geflochten	flicht	flicht	flöchte
s Fließen	flow	floß	gefloſſen	fließt	fließ(e)	flöſſe
Genießen	enjoy	genoß	genoſſen	genießt	genieße	genöſſe
Gießen	pour	goß	gegoſſen	gießt	gieß(e)	göſſe
s Glimmen	glimmer	glomm	geglommen	glimmt	glimm(e)	glömme
Klimmen	climb	klomm	geklommen	klimmt	klimm(e)	klömme
s Kriechen	creep	kroch	gekrochen	kriecht	kriech(e)	kröche
Melken (also weak)	milk	molk	gemolken	milkt	melke	mölke
s Quellen	spring (of water)	quoll	gequollen	quillt	quill	quölle
Riechen	smell	roch	gerochen	riecht	riech(e)	röche
Saufen	drink	ſoff	geſoffen	ſäuft	ſauf(e)	ſöffe
Schallen (also weak)	sound	ſcholl	geſchollen	ſchallt	ſchalle	ſchölle
Schießen	shoot	ſchoß	geſchoſſen	ſchießt	ſchieß(e)	ſchöſſe
Schließen	shut	ſchloß	geſchloſſen	ſchließt	ſchließ(e)	ſchlöſſe
s Schmelzen	melt	ſchmolz	geſchmolzen	ſchmilzt	ſchmilz	ſchmölze
Schwellen	swell	ſchwoll	geſchwollen	ſchwillt	ſchwill	ſchwölle
Sieden (also weak)	boil (trans. or intrans.)	ſott	geſotten	ſiedet	ſied(e)	ſötte
s Sprießen	sprout	ſproß	geſproſſen	ſprießt	ſprieß(e)	ſpröſſe
Triefen (also weak)	drip	troff	getroffen	trieft	trief(e)	tröffe
Verdrießen	vex	verdroß	verdroſſen	verdrießt	verdrieß(e)	verdröſſe

250. Ablaut: ie—ō—ō.

(ii) All these verbs are conjugated exactly like biegen.

Biegen	bend	bog	gebogen	biegt	biege	büge
Bieten	offer	bot	geboten			
s Fliegen	fly	flog	geflogen			
s Fliehen	flee	floß	geflohen			
Frieren	freeze	fror	gefroren			
Kiesen } Küren }	choose	for	gekoren			
Schieben	shove	schob	geschoben			
Stieben	scatter	stob	gestoben			
Verlieren	lose	verlor	verloren			
Wiegen	weigh	wog	gewogen			
Ziehen	draw	zog	gezogen			

251. Also: Ablaut: ē (ä, au, ü)—ō—ō.
All these verbs are regular.

Bewegen	induce	bewog	bewogen	bewegt	bewege	bewöge
Gären	ferment	gor	gegoren			
Lügen	lie	log	gelogen			
Pflegen	practise	pflog	gepflogen			
Saugen	suck	sog	gesogen			
Scheren	shear	schor	geschoren			
Schnauben	snort	schnob	geschnoben			
Trügen	deceive	trog	getrogen			
Wägen	weigh	wog	gewogen			
Weben	weave	wob	gewoben			

252. The following have alternative forms:

Heben	raise	hob or hub	gehoben	hebt	hebe	höbe or hübe
Schwören	swear	schwor or schwur	geschworen	schwört	schwöre	schwüre

253. Group F. Ablaut: ē (ĕ, ĭ, ie)—ā—ē.

Infinitive		Past	Past Participle	3rd sing. Pres. Ind.	Imperative	Past Subj.
Bitten	ask	bat	gebeten	bittet	bitte	bäte
Eſſen	eat	aß	gegeſſen	ißt	iß	äße
Freſſen	eat	fraß	gefreſſen	frißt	friß	fräße
Geben	give	gab	gegeben	gibt	gib	gäbe
s Geneſen	recover	genas	geneſen	geneſt	geneſe	genäſe
s Geſchehen	happen	geſchah	geſchehen	geſchieht	—	geſchähe
Leſen	read	las	geleſen	lieſt	lies	läſe
Liegen	lie	lag	gelegen	liegt	liege	läge
Meſſen	measure	maß	gemeſſen	mißt	miß	mäße
Sehen	see	ſah	geſehen	ſieht	ſieh(e)	ſähe
Sitzen	sit	ſaß	geſeſſen	ſitzt	ſitze	ſäße
s Treten	tread	trat	getreten	tritt	tritt	träte
(also to kick, *trans.* with haben)						
Vergeſſen	forget	vergaß	vergeſſen	vergißt	vergiß	vergäße

254. Group G. Ablaut: ei—ĭ—ĭ.
These verbs are all regular throughout.

Infinitive		Past	Past Participle	3rd sing. Pres. Ind.	Imperative	Past Subj.
(i) Befleißen (ſich)	take pains	befliß	befliſſen	befleißt	befleiße	befliſſe
Beißen	bite	biß	gebiſſen			
s Erbleichen	turn pale	erblich	erblichen			
Gleichen	resemble	glich	geglichen			
s Gleiten	glide	glitt	geglitten			
Greifen	seize	griff	gegriffen			
Kneifen	nip	kniff	gekniffen			
Leiden	suffer	litt	gelitten			
Pfeifen	pipe	pfiff	gepfiffen			
Reißen	tear	riß	geriſſen			
s Reiten	ride	ritt	geritten			
s Schleichen	slink	ſchlich	geſchlichen			

German	English	Past	Past participle
Schleifen	sharpen	schliff	geschliffen
Schmeißen	smite	schmiß	geschmissen
Schneiden	cut	schnitt	geschnitten
s Schreiten	stride	schritt	geschritten
Spleißen	split	spliß	gespliffen
Streichen	stroke	strich	gestrichen
Streiten	quarrel	stritt	gestritten
s Weichen	yield	wich	gewichen

255. Ablaut: ei—ie—ie. These verbs are all regularly conjugated.

German	English	Past	Past participle	Present		
(ii) s Bleiben	remain	blieb	geblieben	bleibt	bleibe	bliebe
Gedeihen	thrive	gedieh	gediehen			
Leihen	lend	lieh	geliehen			
Meiden	avoid	mied	gemieden			
Preisen	praise	pries	gepriesen			
Reiben	rub	rieb	gerieben			
Scheiden	part	schied	geschieden			
Scheinen	shine	schien	geschienen			
Schreiben	write	schrieb	geschrieben			
Schreien	cry	schrie	geschrieen			
Schweigen	be silent	schwieg	geschwiegen			
Speien	spit	spie	gespieen			
s Steigen	climb	stieg	gestiegen			
Treiben	drive	trieb	getrieben			
Weisen	show	wies	gewiesen			
Zeihen	accuse	zieh	geziehen			

256. Group H. The four verbs gehen, stehen, tun and wissen are irregular.

German	English	Past	Past participle	Present		
s Gehen	go	ging	gegangen	geht	geh(e)	ginge
Stehen	stand	stand	gestanden	steht	steh(e)	stände or stünde
Tun	do	tat	getan	tut	tu(e)	täte
Wissen	know	wußte	gewußt	weiß	wiß(e)	wüßte

257. Group I. The following verbs are really weak, the vowel of the present having been modified (Rückumlaut).

Infinitive		Past	Past Participle	3rd sing. Pres. Ind.	Imperative	Past Subj.
Brennen	burn	brannte	gebrannt	brennt	brenne	brennte
Kennen	know	kannte	gekannt	kennt	kenne	kennte
Nennen	name	nannte	genannt			nennte
s Rennen	run	rannte	gerannt			rennte
Senden	send	{ sendete / sandte	{ gesendet / gesandt	All Pres. Ind. and Imperatives regular		sendete
Wenden	turn	{ wendete / wandte	{ gewendet / gewandt			wendete

Also:

Bringen	bring	brachte	gebracht			brächte
Denken	think	dachte	gedacht			dächte
Dünken	seem	{ deuchte / dünkte	{ gedeucht / gedünkt			{ deuchte / dünkte

ALPHABETICAL LIST OF STRONG AND IRREGULAR VERBS.

258.

Backen A

befehlen C iii

befleißen (sich) G i

beginnen C ii

beißen G i

bergen C i

bersten C i

bewegen E ii

bieten E ii

binden D

bitten F

blasen B

bleiben G ii

braten B

brechen C i

brennen I

bringen I

Denken I

dingen D

dreschen C i

dringen D

dünken I

Empfehlen C iii

erbleichen G i

erlöschen E i

erschrecken C i

essen F

Fahren A

fallen B

fangen B

fechten E i

finden D

flechten E i

fliegen E ii

fliehen E ii

fließen E i

fressen F

frieren E ii

Gären E ii

gebären C iii

geben F

gedeihen G ii

gefallen B

gehen H

gelingen D

gelten C i

genesen F

genießen E i

geschehen F

gewinnen C ii

gießen E i

gleichen G i

gleiten G i

glimmen E i

graben A

greifen G i

Halten B

hangen B

hauen B

heben E ii

heißen B

helfen C i

Kennen I

kiesen E ii

klimmen E i

klingen D

kneifen G i

kommen C i

kriechen E i

küren E ii

Laden A

lassen B

laufen B

leiden G i

leihen G ii

lesen F

liegen F

lügen E ii

Meiden G ii

melken E i

messen F

Nehmen C iii

nennen I

Pfeifen G i

pflegen E ii

preisen G ii

Quellen E i

Raten B
reiben G ii
reißen G i
reiten G i
rennen I
riechen E i
ringen D
rinnen C ii
rufen B

Saufen E i
saugen E ii
schaffen A
schallen E i
scheiden G ii
scheinen G ii
schelten C i
scheren E ii
schieben E ii
schießen E i
schinden D
schlafen B
schlagen A
schleichen G i
schleifen G i
schließen E i
schlingen D
schmeißen G i
schmelzen E i
schnauben E ii
schneiden G i

schreiben G ii
schreien G ii
schreiten G i
schweigen G ii
schwellen E i
schwimmen C ii
schwinden D
schwingen D
schwören E ii
sehen F
senden I
sieben E i
singen D
sinken D
sinnen C ii
sitzen F
speien G ii
spinnen C ii
spleißen G i
sprechen C i
sprießen E i
springen D
stechen C i
stecken C i
stehen H
stehlen C iii
steigen G ii
sterben C i
stieben E ii
stinken D
stoßen B
streichen G i
streiten G i

Tragen A
treffen C i
treiben G ii
treten F
triefen E i
trinken D
trügen E ii
tun H

Verderben C i
verdrießen E i
vergessen F
verlieren E ii

Wachsen A
wägen E ii
waschen A
weben E ii
weichen G i
weisen G ii
wenden I
werben C i
werden C i
werfen C i
wiegen E ii
winden D
wissen H

Zeihen G ii
ziehen E ii
zwingen D

Verbs

95

259. THE PASSIVE VOICE (das Passivum).

The Passive is formed by means of werden and the Past Participle. Note especially (i) the order of words, and (ii) the omission of the ge- of geworden in the compound tenses.

Passive of Tragen.

Indicative.	Subjunctive.

PRESENT.

ich werde getragen	ich werde getragen
du wirst getragen	du werdest getragen
er wird getragen	er werde getragen
wir werden getragen	wir werden getragen
ihr werdet getragen	ihr werdet getragen
sie werden getragen.	sie werden getragen.

PAST.

ich wurde getragen.	ich würde getragen.

PERFECT.

ich bin getragen worden.	ich sei getragen worden.

PLUPERFECT.

ich war getragen worden.	ich wäre getragen worden.

FUTURE-PERFECT.

ich werde getragen worden sein.	ich werde getragen worden sein.

FUTURE.

ich werde getragen werden.	ich werde getragen werden.

Conditional.	Conditional-Perfect.
ich würde getragen werden.	ich würde getragen worden sein.

Imperative.

Sing. Werde getragen!   *Plur.* Werdet getragen!   (See § 261.)

Infinitive.

PRESENT. getragen werden.   *PERFECT.* getragen worden sein.

260. Distinguish between the Passive Voice and ſein + Past
Participle:

Die Tür wird um acht Uhr geſchloſſen = Man ſchließt die Tür...
The door is shut at eight o'clock.

Sie kommen zu ſpät; die Tür iſt geſchloſſen.
You come too late; the door is shut.

The former denotes an act, the latter a state.

261. In the Imperative, the form with werden is generally re-
placed by either ſein + Past Participle or laſſen + Reflexive
Pronoun + Active Infinitive:

Seid mir gegrüßt, befreundte Scharen!
I greet you, friendly hosts.

Laſſen Sie ſich nicht betrügen!
Do not be deceived.

262. The agent is expressed by von + Dative:

Dieſe Kur wird von allen Ärzten empfohlen.
This treatment is recommended by all the doctors.

263. Only transitive verbs can form a passive; and the subject
of the passive verb must correspond to the accusative of
the active:

Mir iſt ein Buch gegeben worden.   I have been given a book.

Verbs governing the genitive or dative can form only an
impersonal passive:

Dir wird geholfen; you will be helped.

Deiner ward erwähnt; you were mentioned.

Es wird deiner erinnert; you are remembered.

Dem Mann kann geholfen werden; the man can be helped.

264. Intransitive verbs are also used in the Passive, impersonally:

Es wurde getanzt, geſungen und getrunken.
There was dancing, singing and drinking.

Um wieviel Uhr wird gegeſſen?   What time is dinner?

Cf. the Latin: tres horas pugnatum est.

265. As equivalents of the Passive may be used

  (i) Man: Was sagt man darüber?
                 What is said of it?
                 Man wird dir helfen.
                 You will be helped.

  (ii) A reflexive: Mein Buch hat sich gefunden.
                 My book has been found.

  (iii) Lassen with Er hat sich seit drei Jahren nicht sehen lassen.
      a reflexive: He has not been seen for three years.

  (iv) Gehen is used to form the Passive of verlieren:
                 Sein ganzes Vermögen ist verloren gegangen.
                 All his fortune has been lost.

266. COMPOUND VERBS (zusammengesetzte Zeitwörter).

German possesses a very large number of compound verbs. As in English, these may be written in one word (vergesse, forget) or in two (gehe aus, go out).

In the first class, the Inseparable Compounds, the prefix has so coalesced with the verb, that it has lost its original tonic value, and in many cases seems to add nothing to the meaning of the verb, as in verlieren, vergrößern, besteuern; cf. *awake, arouse, betide*; though in others it has a clear effect on the meaning, as in verkaufen, verlernen; cf. *forgo, forbid.*

In the second class, the Separable Compounds, the fusion is not so complete; the prefix retains its stress accent, and its force can usually be clearly traced, even when the verb is used in a figurative sense:

    ich gehe aus, I go out; ich schreibe nieder, I write down.

We distinguish between three classes of prefix: the Inseparable, the Separable, and the Variable.

267. The Inseparable Prefixes are

    be-, emp-, ent-, er-, ge-, miß-, ver-, zer-, hinter, wider.
Their meanings are discussed in §§ 523, etc.

These are

(i) unstressed; (ii) never separated from the verb-stem;

(iii) never accompanied by the augment ge٭.

In other respects, verbs compounded with them are conjugated exactly like the simple verbs from which they are formed; except that a verb conjugated with ſein may, when compounded, become transitive, in which case the compound verb takes haben.

268. EXAMPLE OF A VERB WITH INSEPARABLE PREFIX.

From   kommen,   kam,   gekommen

is formed bekommen,   bekam,   bekommen, to get (transitive).

Only a few tenses need be given here.

Pres. Ind. ich bekomme,   du bekommſt, er bekommt;
           wir bekommen, ihr bekommt, ſie bekommen.

Past Ind. ich bekam,   du bekamſt, er bekam;
        wir bekamen, ihr bekamt, ſie bekamen.

Fut. Ind. ich werde bekommen, du wirſt bekommen, er wird bekommen, etc.

Perf. Ind. ich habe bekommen, du haſt bekommen, er hat bekommen, etc.

Imperative. Bekomme! Bekommt!

269. The Separable Prefixes are very numerous, including all except those above and those in § 272 below. The most important are:

(i) Adverbs and Prepositions:

ab, off	bei, by	her, hither	vor, before
an, beside	ein, in	hin, thither	weg, away
auf, up	fort, forth	nach, after	zurück, back;
aus, out			

the Compounds vorbei, past; entgegen, towards, etc.; herunter, hinunter, down; and other compounds of hin and her, § 407.

(ii) Nouns:

> teil‹nehmen, to take part; ſchlittſchuh‹laufen, skate; rad‹
> fahren, cycle; ſtatt‹finden, take place.

(iii) Adjectives:

> ſtill‹ſtehen, stop; frei‹ſprechen, acquit; los‹laſſen, release;
> voll‹ſchenken, fill. See § 85.

270. These prefixes

(i) are always stressed;

(ii) always come at the end of the clause, except when the verb itself comes last, in which case the two words are written as one; e.g.

> er kam in London an; als er in London ankam;
> ſtehen Sie ſofort auf! er will nicht aufſtehen.

(iii) allow the augment ge‹ to come between prefix and past participle: aufgeſtanden, angekommen;

and the particle zu to come between prefix and infinitive:

> er hofft, heute anzukommen; er hat keine Luſt, aufzuſtehen.

271. EXAMPLE OF A VERB WITH SEPARABLE PREFIX.

From	kommen,	kam,	gekommen
is formed	ankommen,	kam...an,	angekommen.

Pres. Ind.	ich komme an,	du kommſt an,	er kommt an, etc.
Past Ind.	ich kam an,	du kamſt an,	er kam an, etc.
Perf. Ind.	ich bin angekommen, du biſt angekommen, er iſt ange‹ kommen, etc.		

Pluperfect. ich war angekommen, etc.

Fut. Perf. ich werde angekommen ſein, etc.

Imperative. Komme an! Kommt an!

272. **The Variable Prefixes,** i.e. those which in some compounds are inseparable and in others separable, are durch, über, unter, um. In some cases, the same preposition and the same verb form two distinct compounds, one separable, the other inseparable; e.g.

Er feßte in einem Kahn über.   He crossed (the river) in a boat.
Er überfeßte ben Brief.   He translated the letter.

There is no rigid rule to show whether in any particular compound they are separable or not; but one or two principles are illustrated by the examples below.

(i) When the prefix makes an intransitive verb transitive, or alters the direction of a transitive verb, it is inseparable.

(ii) Durch and um, with a purely adverbial sense, are separable.

(iii) Compounds with a figurative meaning are usually inseparable.

273.

dúrchreifen, to travel straight through, without a stop.

wir reiften von A. bis B. dúrch.

ein Buch dúrchfehen, look carefully through, examine, revise.

einen Plan dúrchfeßen, carry a plan into execution.

er ließ mich dúrch, he let me pass through.

er fchlug fich dúrch, he cut his way through.

durchreifen, *trans.* to travel through.

er hat die Schweiz durchreift.

ein Buch durchféhen, look through, glance at.

Cf. durchblättern.

er hat mir die Hand durchfchóffen, he has shot me through the hand (i.e. hat mir eine Kugel durch die Hand gefchoffen).

die Kugel durchbóhrte ein Brett, the bullet went through a board (i.e. bohrte ein Loch durch ein Brett).

Note that in all the examples in the second column, the Accusative is governed by the durch; whereas in the first column the durch often governs a suppressed noun referring to the obstacle passed.

274.

Separable:

überflíeßen, overflow (*intr.*).

bie Spree fließt über, the Spree overflows.

er warf feinen Mantel über, he slipped on his overcoat.

bie Augen gingen ihm über, his eyes filled with tears.

er ging zum Feinbe über, he went over to the enemy.

überfchnappen (properly of a violin-string slipping over the bridge), to go mad.

Inseparable:

überlégen, consider.

überlaffen Sie bas mir, leave that to me.

ich übernehme bas Kommanbo, I assume command.

er hat einen Fußgänger über‌fahren, he has knocked down a pedestrian.

Denoting excess:

fich übereílen, to be too hasty.

überbiéten, to outbid (at an auction).

Less than ten compounds of über are separable.

275.

unterbringen, to take under one's roof, to shelter.

untergehen, go down.

bie Sonne geht unter, the sun sets.

ber Schwimmer taucht unter, the swimmer dives (down).

wo fomme ich unter? where shall I find shelter?

unterfchieben, substitute.

ein untergefchobenes Teftament, a spurious will (supposititious).

unterbrechen, interrupt.

unterbrücken, suppress, oppress.

unterhalten, entertain.

fich unterhalten, converse, or amuse oneself.

unternehmen, undertake.

ein unternehmenber Mann, an enterprising man.

unterfuchen, investigate.

These are the only separable compounds of unter that are in common use.

276.

umbringen, kill

umfommen, die

umfaffen, enclose

umgeben, surround.

Separable:

er brehte ſich um, he turned round.

er fiel um, he fell down.

er {ſtieß / warf} ſeinen Gegner um, he knocked his opponent down.

umkehren (*intr.*), turn back; (*tr.*) invert.

es iſt gerade umgekehrt, it is exactly the other way round.

er zog (kleidete) ſich um, he changed his clothes.

Um separable denotes turning movement, or change.

Inseparable:

umzingeln, encircle.

wir ſind von Spähern umgeben, we are surrounded by spies.

umarmen, embrace.

umſtricken, entangle.

vom Volke umgafft, surrounded by a gaping crowd.

der Himmel hat ſich umzogen, the sky is overcast.

Um inseparable conveys the idea of surrounding.

277. *Note the following pairs:*

Separable:

überſetzen, to put (some one) across (a river); *intr.* to cross

übergehen, desert

überfahren, cross (a river)

umgehen, to go about, associate (with)

Inseparable:

überſetzen, translate

übergehen, overlook, ignore

überfahren, run over

umgehen, evade.

278. Voll is inseparable, except in

            vollfüllen, vollgießen, fill up

            vollpfropfen, vollſchlagen, cram full.

279. Wider is always inseparable, as in widerſtéhen, resist;

     Wieder is inseparable in wiederhólen, repeat; and in no other verb:

     Kommen Sie bald wieder! Come back soon.

     Wann ſehen wir uns wieder? When shall we meet again?

But   Ich habe es Ihnen wiederholt geſagt.

         I have told you repeatedly.

         Er hat ſeine Ausſage wiederholt.

         He has repeated his statement.

280. Double Prefixes.

  (*a*) With stress on first prefix:

ánvertrauen,	entrust,	vertraute an,	anvertraut.
vórbehalten,	reserve,	behielt vor,	vorbehalten.
zúbereiten,	prepare,	bereitete zu,	zubereitet.

  (*b*) With stress on second prefix:

vorángehen,	go in front,	ging voran,	vorangegangen.
bevórstehen,	be imminent,	stand bevor,	bevorgestanden.
hinúntergehen,	go down,	ging hinunter,	hinuntergegangen.

281. Compound Verbs, consisting of Prefix + Verb, are not to be confused with

  (*a*) **Compound Noun + Verb-ending:**

Frühstück, breakfast:

frühstücken,	to breakfast,	frühstückte,	gefrühstückt.

Handhabe, handle:

handhaben,	to handle,	handhabte,	gehandhabt.

Ratschlag, advice:

ratschlagen,	to deliberate,	ratschlagte,	geratschlagt.

282.

  (*b*) **Prefix +** $\left\{ \begin{matrix} \textbf{Compound Noun} \\ \textbf{or Adjective} \end{matrix} \right\}$ **+ Verb-ending:**

Anspruch, claim:

beanspruchen,	to claim,	beanspruchte,	beansprucht.

Antwort, answer:

verantworten,	to justify,	verantwortete,	verantwortet.

Abschied, parting:

verabschieden,	to dismiss,	verabschiedete,	verabschiedet.

Urteil, verdict:

verurteilen,	to condemn,	verurteilte,	verurteilt.

Antrag, offer:
  beantragen,   to propose,   beantragte,   beantragt.
Anlaß, cause:
  veranlassen,   to cause,   veranlaßte,   veranlaßt.
Nachlässig, negligent:
  vernachlässigen, to neglect,   vernachlässigte, vernachlässigt.
  Note that these verbs are all weak.

AUXILIARY VERBS OF MOOD (modale Hilfszeitwörter).

Können, Dürfen, Mögen, Müssen, Sollen, Wollen.

283. The Pres. Ind. of these verbs is really the Past Tense of
the primitive verbs, whose original present is extinct.
Hence the absence of the suffix *t* in the 3rd pers. sing.,
pres. ind. They are also known as Past-Present (or
Praeterito-Present) Verbs.

284. All these verbs are followed by the infinitive without zu.

285. Wissen, though not an auxiliary, is also a past-present
verb, and is included with können, etc., for purposes of
conjugation.

286. In the Compound Tenses the Past Participles gekonnt,
gedurft, etc., are not used when there is a dependent
infinitive. In their place a participle-form identical
with the present infinitive is used.

Ich habe es nicht finden können. I have not been able to find it.
Sie haben arbeiten müssen.   They have had to work.
But
Wir haben nicht arbeiten wollen, wir haben es gemußt.
We did not want to work; we had to.

287. Heißen, bid, laſſen, ſehen, also omit the ge= of the participle after a dependent infinitive; and hören follows the analogy, as do occasionally fühlen, machen, lehren, lernen. For the use of the infinitive with these verbs see §§ 355–359.

Er hat mich gehen laſſen.	He has let me go.
Wir haben ihn hineingehen ſehen.	We saw him go in.
Ich habe es ſagen hören.	I have heard it said.

THE AUXILIARY VERB OF MOOD Können, *TO BE ABLE.*

288. Principal Parts: können, konnte, gekonnt.

Indicative.	Subjunctive.
	PRESENT.
ich kann	ich könne
du kannſt	du könneſt
er kann	er könne
wir können	wir können
ihr könnt	ihr könnet
ſie können.	ſie können.

	PAST.	
ich konnte		ich könnte
du konnteſt		du könnteſt
er konnte		er könnte
wir konnten		wir könnten
ihr konntet		ihr könntet
ſie konnten.		ſie könnten.

PERFECT.

ich habe gekonnt, etc.	ich habe gekonnt, etc.

PLUPERFECT.

ich hatte gekonnt, etc.	ich hätte gekonnt, etc.

FUTURE-PERFECT.

ich werde gekonnt haben, etc.

Conditional.   Conditional Perfect.
ich würde können, etc.   ich würde gekonnt haben, etc.

Imperative.
None.

Infinitive.
PRESENT. können.   *PERFECT.* gekonnt haben.

Participles.
PRESENT. könnend.   *PAST.* gekonnt.

289. Like können are conjugated
    dürfen, mögen, müssen, sollen, wollen and wissen.

Past Participle:

geburft	gemocht	gemußt	gesollt	gewollt	gewußt

Pres. Ind.

ich darf	mag	muß	soll	will	weiß
du darfst	magst	mußt	sollst	willst	weißt
er darf	mag	muß	soll	will	weiß
wir dürfen	mögen	müssen	sollen	wollen	wissen
ihr dürft	mögt	müßt	sollt	wollt	wißt
sie dürfen	mögen	müssen	sollen	wollen	wissen

Pres. Subj.

ich dürfe	möge	müsse	solle	wolle	wisse
du dürfest	mögest	müssest	sollest	wollest	wissest
er dürfe	möge	müsse	solle	wolle	wisse
etc.	etc.	etc.	etc.	etc.	etc.

Past Ind.

ich durfte	mochte	mußte	sollte	wollte	wußte

Past Subj.

ich dürfte	möchte	müßte	sollte	wollte	wüßte

Perfect Ind.

ich habe gedurft   gemocht   gemußt   gesollt   gewollt   gewußt

Pluperfect Ind.

ich hatte gedurft   gemocht   gemußt   gesollt   gewollt   gewußt

Pluperfect Subj.

ich hätte gedurft   gemocht   gemußt   gesollt   gewollt   gewußt

All the Compound Tenses are regular.

Wissen has Imperative Wisse! Wißt!
The others have no Imperative.

USE OF THE AUXILIARIES OF MOOD.

290. The following tables give the commonest uses of these
verbs, and show to some extent the effect of mood and
tense on their meaning.

I. Present Indicative.

Ich kann es lesen		I can read it.
„ darf „		I am permitted to read it.
„ mag „		I like reading it.
„ muß „		I have to read it.
„ soll „		I am to read it.
„ will „		I will read it. / I want to read it.

291. II. Past Indicative.

Ich konnte es lesen		I was able to read it.
„ durfte „		I was allowed to read it.
„ mochte „		I liked reading it.
„ mußte „		I had to read it.
„ sollte „		I was to read it.
„ wollte „		I wanted to read it.

292. III. Past Subjunctive.

Ich könnte es lesen	I could read it (if I tried).
„ dürfte „	I should be allowed to read it.
„ möchte „	I should like to read it.
„ müßte „	I should have to read it.
„ sollte „	I ought to read it.
„ wollte „	I should like to read it.

293. IV. Pluperfect Subjunctive.

Ich hätte es lesen können	I could have read it.
„ „ dürfen	I should have been allowed to read it.
„ „ mögen	I should have liked to read it.
„ „ müssen	I should have had to read it.
„ „ sollen	I ought to have read it.
„ „ wollen	I should have liked to read it.

294. FURTHER (MORE IDIOMATIC) USES OF THE AUXILIARIES OF MOOD.

Können:

Kann ich bleiben?	May I stay?
Ich kann nicht mehr.	I am tired out.
Ich kann nicht anders.	I cannot do otherwise.
Ich kann nichts dafür.	I can't help it.
Das kann ich nicht.	I can't do that.
Er konnte nicht umhin, zu lachen.	He couldn't help laughing.
Er kann gut Französisch.	He is good at French.
Könnten Sie mir sagen...?	Could you tell me...?
Er kann uns gesehen haben.	He may (possibly) have seen us.

295. Dürfen:

Darf ich Sie um das Brot bitten?	May I ask you for the bread?
Sie dürfen nicht zögern.	You must not hesitate.
Das dürfte wohl geschehen.	It will probably happen.

296. Mögen:

Es mag sein.	It *may* be true.
Er mag sagen } was er will. Er sage }	He may } say what he likes. Let him }
Sie mögen alle kommen!	Let them all come!
Sage ihm, er möge zu mir kommen!	Ask him to come to me.
Es möge ihm wohl bekommen!	Much good may it do him!
Ich mag den Mann nicht (leiden).	I don't like the man.
Ich mag nicht Karten spielen.	I don't care to play cards.
Ich möchte wohl wissen.	I should like to know.
Ich habe es nicht tun mögen.	I did not like to do it.

297. Müssen:

Wir müssen nach Hause.	We must go home.
Sie mußten beide sterben.	They were both doomed to die.
Ich mußte lachen.	I could not help laughing.
Er muß wohl krank sein.	He must be ill. I suppose he is ill.
Er muß krank gewesen sein.	He must have been ill.

298. Sollen:

Du sollst nicht töten.	Thou shalt do no murder.
Was soll ich sagen?	What shall I say?
Ich weiß nicht, was ich tun soll.	I don't know what to do.
Hoch soll er leben!	Long may he live! ("For he's a jolly good fellow.")
Sagen Sie ihm, er soll(e) sofort kommen!	Tell him to come at once.
Sollte er dies getan haben...	Should he have done this... (*conditional*).
Er soll in Amerika gestorben sein.	He is said to have died in America.
Was soll das (heißen)?	What does this mean?
Man sollte meinen, er sei verwundet.	One might think he was wounded.
Er soll nach Hamburg.	He is to go to Hamburg.

299. Wollen:

Ich will nicht gehorchen.	I will not obey.
Wo wollen Sie hin?	Where are you going?
Die Sache will nicht vom Fleck.	The affair is not progressing.
Er will durchaus bezahlen.	He insists on paying.
Er hat nicht mitkommen wollen.	He refused to come.
Was wollen Sie damit sagen?	What do you mean by that?
Er mag wollen oder nicht.	Willy nilly.
Wollte Gott, er wäre gesund!	Would to God he were well!
Das wollte ich meinen!	So I should think!
Er $\{{\text{will} \atop \text{wollte}}\}$ eben abfahren.	He $\{{\text{is} \atop \text{was}}\}$ just going to start.
Es scheint regnen zu wollen.	It looks as if it were going to rain.
Sie wollen ihn gesehen haben.	They maintain that they have seen him.

REFLEXIVE VERBS (reflexive Zeitwörter).

300. The conjugation of a reflexive verb does not differ from that of an ordinary verb, with the addition of the reflexive pronoun.

All reflexives are conjugated with haben in the compound tenses.

301. Some verbs are always or normally reflexive; the commonest of these are:

sich	enthalten	to abstain
„	bemühen	„ take trouble
„	entschließen	„ resolve
„	erbarmen	„ pity
„	besinnen	„ recollect
„	schämen	„ be ashamed
„	sehnen	„ long (for)

ſich wundern	to wonder
„ beklagen	„ complain
„ betragen	„ behave
„ nähern	„ approach
„ befinden	„ be (French, *se trouver*).

302. Others are only occasionally reflexive, e.g.

ſich freuen	to rejoice
„ ſetzen	„ sit down
„ verlaſſen (auf)	„ rely (upon)
„ waſchen	„ wash one's self.

303. Many intransitive verbs can be used reflexively in connection with a predicative adjective:

ſich müde gehen,	to tire one's self by walking.
er hat ſich tot gearbeitet,	he has worked himself to death.
Cf. er hat ſich ſatt gegeſſen,	he has eaten his fill.

304. Some compounds in ver= are used reflexively:

ich habe mich verlaufen,	I have lost my way.
„ „ verrechnet,	I have miscalculated.
„ „ verſchrieben,	it was a slip of the pen.
„ „ verſprochen,	it was a slip of the tongue.
„ „ verſungen,	I have sung a false note.
„ „ verſpielt,	I have played a false note.

305. Verbs governing the Dative can also be used reflexively:

ich bilde mir ein,	I fancy.
„ nehme mir vor,	I intend (purpose).
„ ſchmeichle mir,	I flatter myself.
„ ſtelle mir vor,	I imagine.
(but: „ ſtelle mich vor,	I introduce myself.)

IMPERSONAL VERBS (unperſönliche Zeitwörter).

306. These are of three kinds:

    (*a*) Verbs essentially impersonal;
    (*b*) Verbs occasionally impersonal;
    (*c*) Verbs apparently impersonal.

307. (*a*) Verbs essentially impersonal are used only in the 3rd person singular, and can have no subject other than the impersonal pronoun es. To this class belong:

es regnet,	it rains,	es ſchneit,	it snows,
„ hagelt,	„ hails,	„ friert,	„ freezes,
„ donnert,	„ thunders,	„ taut,	„ thaws;
„ blitzt,	„ lightens,		

es dürſtet mich,	I am thirsty,	es ſchläfert mich,	I am sleepy,
„ hungert mich,	„ hungry,	„ wundert mich,	I wonder,
„ graut mir,	I shudder,	„ träumt mir,	I dream.
„ ſchwindelt mir,	I am dizzy,		

308. (*b*) Verbs occasionally impersonal are:

es läutet, „ klingelt, } the bell rings,	es geht mir gut, I am well,
„ ſchlägt, the clock strikes,	„ fehlt mir (an), I need,
„ iſt, there is,	„ brauſt, there is a roaring,
„ ſind, there are,	„ wird getanzt (impersonal passive), there is dancing,
„ gibt, there is (are),	„ kommt darauf an, ob, it depends whether.

309. (*c*) Verbs apparently impersonal are:

es gelingt mir,	I succeed,	es mißlingt mir,	I fail,
„ ärgert mich,	I am angry,	„ fällt mir ein,	it occurs to me,
„ freut mich,	I am glad,	„ kränkt mich,	it offends me,
„ trägt ſich zu, daß, } happens	„ tut mir leid,	I am sorry,
„ geſchieht, daß, } that,	„ verdrießt mich,	I am vexed.

With these verbs the es stands for, or anticipates, a baß-clause or an infinitive, which is the real subject:

> Es ist mir gelungen, meine Prüfung zu bestehen.
> I have succeeded in passing my examination.
>
> Es ärgert mich, daß ich kein Geld habe.
> I am annoyed that I have no money.

310. When the impersonal verb governs a case, the object sometimes precedes; es is then omitted:

> Mich dürstet; mich hungert; mir graut; mir fällt ein.

311. Es gibt, es ist.

Generally speaking, the difference is that es ist is modified by some indication of place, whereas es gibt, which governs the Acc., is used without such limitation:

> Was gibt es zu essen? What is there to eat?
>
> Es gibt nichts schöneres als dies.
> There is nothing finer than this.
>
> Es gibt Regen. There is rain coming.
>
> Es hat Schläge gegeben. There has been a fight.
>
> Es ist ein Loch in deinem Strumpfe.
> There's a hole in your stocking.
>
> Es waren auch Damen dabei.
> There were also ladies present.
>
> Es ist eine Maus unter dem Tische.
> There is a mouse under the table.

Note:
> Es war einmal... Once upon a time there was...

312. Sentences with es ist can usually be inverted so that the es, which is redundant, disappears:

> In deinem Strumpfe ist ein Loch; dabei waren auch Damen.

313. This use of es, as preparatory or *Formal Subject*, is common with other verbs, e.g.

> Es ſtand in alten Zeiten ein Schloß.
> In olden times there stood a castle.
> Es fuhren drei Burſche wohl über den Rhein.
> There were three lads who crossed the Rhine.
> Es ſteht ein Baum im Odenwald.
> In the Odenwald there stands a tree.

CONCORD OF THE VERB (die Übereinſtimmung).

314. Certain cases present difficulty:

(*a*) The forms of courtesy relating to the second person; see §§ 170, 171, 172.

315. (*b*) A collective noun generally takes a singular verb:

> Die Regierung hat beſchloſſen....
> The Government has decided....

But when it denotes an indefinite number and is followed by a genitive plural, a plural verb is preferred:

> Eine Menge Gäſte ſind angekommen.
> A crowd of guests have arrived.
> Ein paar Leute ſind umgekommen.
> A few people perished.

But:

> Ein Paar dieſer Schuhe koſtet 45 Mark.
> A pair of these shoes costs 45 marks.

Other common collective nouns are: die Anzahl, number; der Haufe, heap, crowd; die Schar, host; das Volk, people; das Dutzend, dozen.

316. (*c*) Two or more singular nouns, in close connection, usually take a singular verb; when they suggest two distinct ideas, the verb is in the plural:

> Dein iſt das Reich und die Kraft und die Herrlichkeit.
> Thine is the Kingdom, the Power, and the Glory.

Geld und Gut macht nicht glücklich.
Great possessions do not make men happy.
Haus und Hof ist verkauft.
Everything is sold.

But:

Haus und Garten sind verkauft.
The house and garden are sold. (Two separate things.)

317. (d) When two or more nouns are connected by

sowohl......als auch	both......and
nicht nur......sondern auch	not only......but also
teils......teils	partly......partly
nicht......sondern	not......but
entweder......oder	either......or
weder......noch	neither......nor

the verb agrees in number with the nearer:

Sowohl die Freude, als der Schmerz vergeht.
Both joy and pain are fleeting.

Weder mein Bruder, noch meine Schwestern waren da.
Neither my brother nor my sisters were there.

318. (e) In stating arithmetical facts, the singular is always used:

Zweimal zwei ist vier. $2 \times 2 = 4$.
Drei Viertel von zwanzig ist fünfzehn. $\frac{3}{4}$ of $20 = 15$.

319. (f) The verb agrees with the real, and not with the grammatical subject in such sentences as:

Das bin ich gewesen. Das waren meine Freunde.
That was I. Those were my friends.

Note also:

Ich bin es. It is I. Sind Sie es? Is it you?

320. (*g*) When there are two or more subjects of different persons, joined by unb, the verb is in the First Person if one of the subjects is in the First Person; otherwise it stands in the Second. In such cases the subject is usually resumed, as in French, by a personal pronoun in the plural:

Ich und du find alte Freunde.
Ich und du, wir find alte Freunde.
     You and I are old friends.

Du und dein Freund, ihr werdet bei mir übernachten.

You and your friend will sleep at my house.

321. (*h*) When the subjects are contrasted, or mutually exclusive, the verb agrees with the nearest:

Weder ich, noch du kannst ihm helfen.

Neither you nor I can help him.

Entweder du, oder ich bin verrückt.

Either you or I must be mad.

Nicht ich, fondern du bift undankbar.

It is not I, but you, who are ungrateful.

It is better however in such cases to turn the sentence when possible:

Entweder bift du verrückt, oder ich bin es.

Nicht ich bin undankbar, fondern du.

MOODS (der Mobus, pl. Mobi).

322. The Indicative (der Indikativ).

The Indicative is used in principal sentences to express a statement, question, or exclamation, and in subordinate clauses, where there is no reason for using another mood:

Es war einmal ein König.   There was once a king.

Haft du das Schloß gefehen?   Hast thou seen the castle?

Wie schön ift heut' die Welt!   How fair is the world to-day!

Ich weiß nicht, was foll es bedeuten,

     Daß ich fo traurig bin.

I know not what it meaneth, that I am so sad.

323. The Imperative (der Imperativ).

The Imperative is used only in principal sentences. Strictly speaking, it has only one person, the second; but it forms the other persons by borrowing from the present subjunctive and using auxiliaries. It cannot have a first person singular.

Sing. —	*Plur.* Seien wir vorsichtig!
	Let us be cautious.
Sei vorsichtig!	Seid (Seien Sie) vorsichtig!
Be cautious.	Be cautious.
Er sei vorsichtig!	Sie seien vorsichtig!
Let him be cautious.	Let them be cautious.

Substitutes for the Imperative.

324. (*a*) Sollen, wollen, mögen, and lassen are used to form periphrastic imperatives:

Du sollst nicht töten.	Thou shalt not kill.
Er mag sich nur vorsehen!	Let him be careful.
Heute wollen wir energisch sein!	Let's be energetic to-day.
Laßt uns beten!	Let us pray.

325. (*b*) The Infinitive:

Nicht hinauslehnen!	Don't lean out.
Das Bajonett aufsetzen!	Fix bayonets.

326. (*c*) The Past Participle:

Angetreten!   Fall in!
Nur um des Himmels willen nicht gelacht!
Only, for Heaven's sake, don't laugh.

327. (*d*) The Present or Future Indicative:

Du gehst voran!   You go first.
Ihr werdet um drei Uhr angreifen.
You will attack at three o'clock.

328. (*e*) Various nouns, adjectives, adverbs, interjections:

> Fertig! Feuer! Ready! Fire!
> Auf! Marsch! Marsch!   Rise up! Double (march)!

329. THE SUBJUNCTIVE (der Konjunktiv).

Broadly speaking, the Indicative states a fact, while the Subjunctive states an idea, which may be realised at some future time, or on the other hand may be impossible of realisation. The uses of the Subjunctive may conveniently be grouped under three heads: Optative, expressing a wish; Potential, expressing possibility, and Dependent, expressing a reported statement. The Optative and Potential Subjunctives are found both in main sentences and in subordinate clauses.

Optative Subjunctive.

330. (*a*) *In the Present*, to express a wish capable of fulfilment:

> Gott sei uns gnädig! God have mercy on us!
> Möge ich das nicht erleben! May I not live to see that!

In Noun Clauses the Imperfect may also be used in this sense, when the main verb is in the Past:

> Ich wünschte, daß Sie es erführen.
> I wished you to find it out.

331. Sometimes the Wish becomes a Command (Jussive):

> Es werde Licht! Let there be light.
> Es kämpfe jeder seine Schlacht allein!
> Let each man fight his own battle.

332. From this, again, is derived the Concessive use of the Subjunctive:

> Es koste, was es wolle! No matter what it costs.
> Es komme, was da kommen mag! Come what may.
> Dem sei, wie es wolle! Be that as it may.

333. (b) *In the Past or the Pluperfect*, to express a wish unlikely to be fulfilled, or incapable of fulfilment:

Wollte Gott, ich wär' heute bei ihr!
Would God I were with her to-day!
O wär' ich nie geboren! O that I had never been born!
O hätt' ich nie gelebt, um das zu schau'n!
O that I had never lived to see that sight!

Potential Subjunctive.

334. (a) *In Conditional Sentences*, where the fulfilment of the condition is regarded as improbable or impossible, the Past or Pluperfect Subjunctive is used in both parts:

Ich wäre froh, wenn ich gesund wäre.
I should be happy if I were well.
Wären Sie früher angekommen, so hätten Sie alles gesehen.
If you had arrived earlier, you would have seen everything.

Often with ellipse of the Protasis:

Es hätte mich gefreut, Sie zu begrüßen.
It would have given me great pleasure to welcome you.

335. Note that the Present Subjunctive is not used in Conditional Sentences:

If this *be* true, ... Wenn dies der Fall ist, ...

336. (b) *The Subjunctive of Modest Assertion*, perhaps with ellipse of a conditional clause:

Ich wüßte wohl, was zu tun wäre.
I think I know what is to be done.
Jetzt wären wir vollzählig. Now we are all present, I think.

Sometimes expressing incredulity, real or feigned:

Das wären Sie! Do you mean to say that it is *you*!

This use is especially common with the auxiliaries of mood:

Es dürfte heute regnen. It will probably rain to-day.
Ich möchte gern wissen. I should like to know.
Dürfte ich Sie um Feuer bitten?
May I ask you for a match?

337. (c) *In Comparative and Concessive Clauses* of Conditional type:

Er sah aus, { als wenn (als ob) er nicht geschlafen hätte.
           als hätte er nicht geschlafen.
           als habe er nicht geschlafen.

He looked as if he had not slept.

Wir folgen dir, und wenn's zur Hölle ginge.

We'll follow you, though it should be to Hell.

The Indicative is also used in Concessive Clauses:

Gedulb, Gedulb, wenn's Herz auch bricht!

Patience, patience, though thy heart is breaking.

See §§ 576, 581.

338. (d) *In Relative Clauses*, suggesting what *might* happen:

Da ist der Kahn, der mich hinübertrüge.

There is the boat that would bear me across (the lake).

Cf. Nicht daß ich wüßte. Not so far as I know; and see § 570 (b).

339. (e) *In Final Clauses:*

Er versteckte sich, damit wir ihn nicht sähen.

He hid in order that we might not see him.

But in Present Time the Indicative is commonly used instead of the Subjunctive:

Ich will mich verstecken, damit er mich nicht sieht.

I will hide, so that he may not see me.

340. *Note in the above examples that the Potential use of the Subjunctive is confined to the Imperfect and Pluperfect. The only exceptions are comparative clauses (§ 337) and final clauses (§ 339); and even there the use of the Present (or Perfect) Subjunctive is not necessary.*

Dependent Subjunctive.

341. *In Indirect Statements*, i.e. after verbs of saying, thinking, knowing, etc., the Indicative is used to express a fact which is considered by the speaker to be true:

Es ist wahr, daß er lahm ist. It is true that he is lame.

Ich weiß, daß er nicht kommt. I know he is not coming.

Ich glaube, es hat zwei geschlagen. I think it has struck two.

342. The Subjunctive is used in statements which are not given as the personal opinion of the speaker:

Er sagt, er sei krank.

He says he is ill (which may, or may not, be true).

Die Jungen meinen, wir alten seien sehr unschuldig.

The boys think we old men are very innocent (but we are not).

343. *In Indirect Questions* the Indicative is generally used of present time, the Subjunctive of past time:

Sage mir, mit wem er umgeht! Tell me who his friends are.

Ich fragte ihn, was er in der Küche mache.

I asked him what he was doing in the kitchen.

344. *In Indirect Command* use sollen or mögen; mögen is the more polite:

Sagen Sie dem Müller, er soll(e) sofort hierher kommen!

Tell Müller to come here at once.

Ich werde den Herrn Direktor bitten, er möge mir meine Strafe erlassen.

I shall ask the Headmaster to let me off my punishment.

TENSES OF THE SUBJUNCTIVE.

345. Generally, German uses the same tense as English. But there is an important exception, namely Indirect Speech. Here the rule is the same as that which governs the tense of the Infinitive in Oratio Obliqua in Latin;

the verb is Present, Past or Future according as it would have been Present, Past or Future in the original Direct Speech. It is therefore advisable for beginners, when translating from English into German, to transpose such sentences into Direct Speech, before turning them into German.

Examples:

He said he *was* ill. Turning this into Direct Speech, we get: He said: "I *am* ill." This goes into German: Er sagte: „Ich bin krank." In Indirect Speech: Er sagte, er sei krank.

He said he *was* working.   He said: "I *am* working."
Er sagte: „Ich arbeite."   Er sagte, er arbeite.

He says he *has been* working.   He says: "I *have been* working."
Er sagt: „Ich habe gearbeitet."   Er sagt, er habe gearbeitet.

He said he *would work* hard.   He said: "I *will work* hard."
     Er sagte: „Ich werde fleißig arbeiten."
     Er sagte, er werde fleißig arbeiten.

Similarly with Future-Perfect time:

     He will have finished his work before you return.
     Er wird mit seiner Arbeit fertig geworden sein, usw.

becomes:

Er sagt, ⎫
Er sagte, ⎬ er werde mit seiner Arbeit fertig geworden sein, usw.

346. *Note.* (i) The tense of the governing verb makes no difference to that of the governed:

Er glaubt, ⎫
Er wird glauben, ⎬ wir seien krank.
Er glaubte, ⎭

347.   (ii) The Imperfect Subjunctive is not used in Indirect Speech, except as in (iii) below. 'Do you think he did it?' is in German: Meinen Sie, er habe es getan?

Verbs 123

348. (iii) Where the Present Subjunctive has the same form as the Present Indicative (e.g. Pres. Ind. id) **habe**; Pres. Subj. id) **habe**), the Imperfect Subjunctive is used instead of the Present:

Er ſagt, ich hätte (not ich habe) unrecht.
He says I am wrong.

Er fragte, ob wir mitgehen wollten (not wollen).
He asked whether we would go with him.

Similarly, in the compound tenses:

Sie ſagten, ſie hätten fleißig gearbeitet.
They said they had worked hard.

Sie ſagten, ſie würden fleißig arbeiten.
They said they would work hard.

349. (iv) Where the verb of saying is in parenthesis, the verb of Reported Speech is still in the Subjunctive:

Die Bäume ſeien gebannt, ſagt er.
The trees are enchanted, he says.

THE CONDITIONAL (der Konditionalis).

350. This name is given to certain forms which really belong to the Subjunctive. There are two distinct uses of the Conditional:

351. (a) **In Indirect Speech,** where the required forms of the Future (or Future-Perfect) Subjunctive would not be distinguishable from the Indicative:

Direct: Sie werden nicht ſingen. They will not sing.

Indirect: Sie ſagten, ſie würden nicht ſingen.

Direct: Sie werden binnen zwei Stunden fertig geworden ſein.
They will have finished within two hours.

Indirect: Sie ſagten, ſie würden...fertig geworden ſein.

352. (*b*) **In a Main Sentence,** with an improbable condition expressed or implied, as in § 334 above; in such sentences it is equivalent to the Imperfect (or Pluperfect) Subjunctive:

Probable Condition:

    Ich werde froh sein, wenn es dir gelingt.
    I shall be glad if you succeed.

Improbable Condition:

    Ich würde froh sein,⎫
 or Ich wäre froh,   ⎬ wenn es dir gelänge.
    I should be glad if you were to succeed.

Impossible Condition:

    Ich würde froh gewesen sein,⎫
 or Ich wäre froh gewesen,   ⎬ wenn es dir gelungen wäre.
    I should have been glad if you had succeeded.

353. N.B. (i) The Conditional is used in the *Main Sentence,* and not in the wenn-clause.

    'If it should rain,'

is therefore not, in German, Wenn es regnen würde,

but Wenn es regnete, or Wenn es regnen sollte.

    If you would come and see us, we should be delighted.
    Wenn Sie uns besuchten, usw.
 or Wenn Sie uns besuchen wollten, usw.

354. N.B. (ii) *Would,* in English, often stands for 'was accustomed'; in this sense its German equivalent is pflegte, or the plain Past tense may be used:

    He would often tell me fairy tales.
    Oft erzählte er mir Märchen.

Sometimes, too, *would* means 'insisted'; and still more frequently, *would not* means 'refused':

Er hat mich nicht anhören wollen.
He would not listen to me.

Du bist selber daran schuld; du hast durchaus mitkommen wollen.
It is your own fault; you *would* come with us.

THE INFINITIVE (ber Infinitiv).

355. The Infinitive is used without zu

(*a*) **As a Verbal Noun,** especially with the Article:

Das Wandern ist des Müllers Lust.
The miller's joy is roving.

Ich bin des Treibens müde.
I am weary of wandering.

Sometimes without the Article:

(i) in Proverbs:

Reden ist Silber, Schweigen ist Gold.
Speech is silver; silence is gold.

(ii) after nennen and heißen:

Das heiß' ich gut einkaufen.
I call that a good bargain.

Das heißt eine Katze im Sack kaufen!
That's what I call buying a pig in a poke.

356. (*b*) **After the Auxiliaries of Mood:**

Wollen Sie nicht bleiben?   Won't you stay?

357. (*c*) **After lehren, lernen, lassen, heißen (bid):**

Er lehrt mich schwimmen.   He teaches me to swim.
Er hieß uns schweigen.   He bade us be quiet.

358. N.B. After laſſen the Infinitive may have either an active or a passive meaning:

> Laſſen Sie mich ſprechen! Let me speak.
>
> Laſſen Sie ſich nicht erwiſchen! Don't be found out.
>
> Er läßt ſich das Haar ſchneiden. He gets his hair cut.
>
> Ich ließ ihn rufen means *either* I let him shout,
>
> > *or* I had him called.

359. (*d*) **With the sense of the Present Participle:**

(i) *After Transitive Verbs*, e.g. ſehen, hören, fühlen:

> Wir hörten ihn rufen. We heard him calling.
>
> Ich ſah ihn ſterben. I saw him die.
>
> Er hat Geld im Kaſten liegen. He has money lying in his coffers.

(ii) *After Intransitives*, especially in the phrases

> ſitzen, ſtehen, liegen bleiben, to sit, stand, or lie still;
>
> ſpazieren gehen, reiten, fahren, to go for a walk, ride, or drive.

360. (*e*) *As an Imperative:*

> Alles ausſteigen! All change!

361. **The Infinitive with zu is used**

(*a*) **To complete the meaning of a Noun, Adjective, or Verb:**

> Er ſann auf Mittel, ſich zu rächen.
>
> He tried to find a way to avenge himself.
>
> Ich ergreife die Gelegenheit, Ihnen zu danken.
>
> I seize the opportunity of thanking you.
>
> Die Kunſt, zu gefallen. The art of pleasing.
>
> Das iſt leicht zu erraten. That is easy to guess.
>
> Ich bin bereit, dieſe Summe zu bezahlen.
>
> I am prepared to pay this sum.
>
> Es fängt an, zu regnen. It is beginning to rain.
>
> Er bat mich, zu ſchreiben. He bade me write.
>
> Er fürchtet zu mißfallen. He is afraid of giving offence.

362. (*b*) **In Apposition to the impersonal** es, **or to the** da **in** daran, darin, **etc.** :

Es ist unmöglich, alles zu wissen.

It is impossible to know everything.

Es freut mich, Sie wiederzusehen.   I am glad to see you again.

Er bestand darauf, in die Küche zu gehen.

He insisted on going into the kitchen.

Note. This use of the Infinitive is admissible only when it has the same subject as the governing verb. In other cases a daß-clause must be used (see § 377):

Er bestand darauf, daß ich in die Küche ginge.

363. (*c*) **After** ohne, statt, anstatt, um :

Wie kann man reich werden, ohne zu arbeiten?

How can you grow rich without working?

Statt seine alten Schulden zu bezahlen, macht er neue.

Instead of paying his old debts, he is contracting new ones.

Der Mensch lebt nicht, um zu essen, sondern er ißt, um zu leben.

Man does not live to eat, but eats to live.

Note. Here again the Infinitive is not admissible when there is a change of subject:

Er ist reich geworden, ohne daß ich's merkte.

He has grown rich without my noticing it.

364. (*d*) **As a Passive Participle (Gerundive) after** sein **and** bleiben :

Dieses Haus ist $\begin{cases} \text{zu vermieten.} \\ \text{zu verkaufen.} \end{cases}$ This house is $\begin{cases} \text{to be let.} \\ \text{to be sold.} \end{cases}$

Meine Schwester ist nirgends zu finden.

My sister is nowhere to be found.

Der Mann ist nicht auszustehen.   The man is insufferable.

Es bleibt nichts zu wünschen übrig.

Nothing more could be desired.

Note also:

Dieſer Aufſatz läßt viel zu wünſchen übrig.
This essay leaves much to be desired.

(Cf. French: laisse beaucoup à désirer.)

365. Hence the attributive use of zu + Infinitive as a Gerundive:

Ein zu lobender Schüler. A pupil deserving to be praised.
Ein zu vermietendes Haus. A house to let.
Ein zu verkaufendes Haus. A house for sale.

THE PARTICIPLES (das Partizipium, pl. Partizipien).

366. The Present and Past Participles may have a purely adjectival meaning, in which case they are treated exactly like other adjectives:

Eine brennende Frage. A burning question.
Ein Rock von brennendem Rot. A coat of flaming red.
Eine reizende Landſchaft. A charming landscape.

Similarly raſend, furious; dringend, urgent; bindend, binding; drohend, threatening; entzückend, delightful; verrückt, mad, etc. For Comparison of participles, see § 136.

367. They may be half-adjective, half-verb; in which case they take the usual adjective-endings when they stand immediately before their noun, but are indeclinable in other positions:

Die kunſtlos um den Kopf hängenden Haare....
His hair, which hung artlessly around his head....
Eine alte, ſchwarzgerauchte Pfeife.
An old pipe, black with use.
Die heute angekommenen Gäſte.
The guests who arrived to-day.

Das graue, nur durch seine Größe, nicht durch äußeren Schmuck
sich auszeichnende Haus.

The grey house, which was distinguished only by its size,
and not by any external adornment.

Ein weißer Turban, reich mit Gold gestickt, bedeckte das Haupt.
A white turban, richly embroidered with gold, covered
his head.

Er ritt ein schönes arabisches Pferd, mit einer Tigerdecke behängt.
He rode a fine Arab horse, decked with a saddle-rug of
tiger-skin.

368. The Present Participle, unless purely adjectival, cannot
be used as the complement of sein or bleiben. While it is
correct to say: die Landschaft ist reizend, the landscape is
charming; der Brief ist dringend, the letter is urgent;
der General war rasend, the general was furious; we cannot say: das Kind war schlafend, still less: die Haare
waren ihm um den Kopf hängend.

These must be rendered:

das Kind schlief; die Haare hingen ihm um den Kopf.

369. But Past Participles of transitive verbs can always be
used as the complement of sein:

Die Pfeife ist schwarzgeraucht. The pipe is black with use.

370. The Participles may be used adverbially, either as simple
adverbs:

Sie hat reizend gesungen. She sang charmingly;

or to form short clauses:

Schwer betroffen sinkt er nieder.
Sorely wounded he sinks to the earth.

Ich fand den jungen Mann, der, noch immer das Buch in der Hand haltend, gedankenvoll umherging.

I found the young man, who was walking about in meditation,.still holding the book in his hand.

371. The Present Participle in this construction is much less common in German than in English, and should never be used to express cause, nor may it be used in cases where the two acts are not simultaneous.

'Standing on one foot, he counted a hundred,' may be rendered: Auf einem Fuße stehend, usw. But, 'Sitting down at the writing table, he began to write,' is, in German, Er setzte sich an den Schreibtisch und fing an zu schreiben, or Nachdem er sich... gesetzt hatte, fing er an...

Having no money myself, I can't lend you any.

Da ich selber kein Geld habe, so kann ich Ihnen keines leihen.

Feeling unwell, he stayed at home.

Da er sich unwohl fühlte, so blieb er zu Hause.

372. Note the use of the Past Participle after kommen:

Er kommt (kam) gelaufen, geritten, geflogen, gefahren, usw.

He comes (came) running, riding, flying, driving, etc.; also very frequently hergelaufen, hergefahren, herbeigeeilt, usw. These participles of verbs conjugated with sein have an active meaning. Past participles of verbs which take haben cannot be used in the same way, their meaning being passive. Thus we can say er kam singend, but not er kam gesungen.

373. The Participles are used as Nouns:

Der Reisende, the traveller; die Anwesenden, those present; die Umstehenden, the bystanders; die Vorübergehenden, the passers-by; das Unbegrenzte, the infinite; das Gewünschte, the thing desired; ein Gefrorenes, an ice.

THE ENGLISH GERUND AND PRESENT PARTICIPLE.

374. The **Gerund** is a Verbal Noun and is rendered in German

(*a*) **By the Definite Article + Infinitive:**

The whining of the dog. Das Winseln des Hundes.
The reading of the Bible. Das Lesen der Bibel.
Boxing is a manly sport. Das Boxen ist ein männlicher Sport.
N.B. I don't like dancing. Ich tanze nicht gern.

375. (*b*) **By a daß-clause:**

Your coming to see us was most fortunate.
Es war sehr glücklich, daß Sie uns besuchten.

376. (*c*) **After a Preposition:**

(i) when the subject is the same as that of the main verb, usually by zu + Infinitive; otherwise (ii) by a daß-clause; see §§ 361, 566.

(i) I have not the honour of knowing you.
Ich habe nicht die Ehre, Sie zu kennen.
Instead of obeying me, he went on singing.
Statt mir zu gehorchen, sang er ruhig weiter.
I insist on getting up at once.
Ich bestehe darauf, sofort aufzustehen.

377. (ii) I insist on your getting up at once.
Ich bestehe darauf, daß Sie sofort aufstehen.
Do you object to my smoking?
Haben Sie etwas dagegen, daß ich rauche?
I know nothing about his being ill.
Ich weiß nichts davon, daß er krank sei.
I rely on your being punctual.
Ich verlasse mich darauf, daß Sie pünktlich kommen.
I offended him by telling him the truth.
Ich kränkte ihn dadurch, daß ich ihm die Wahrheit sagte.

378. **The English Present Participle** may be translated into German

(*a*) **By the Present Participle,** but only when the act it expresses is simultaneous with that expressed by the main verb:

Eine Zigarette rauchend, las er den neuesten Roman.

Smoking a cigarette, he was reading the latest novel.

See §§ 370, 371.

379. (*b*) **By a da-clause:**

The door being open, he went in.

Da die Tür offen stand, so trat er hinein.

Being hungry, he ordered a portion of roast beef.

Da er hungrig war, bestellte er eine Portion Roastbeef.

380. (*c*) **By a Relative Clause:**

There's a squirrel eating a nut.

Da ist ein Eichhörnchen, das eine Nuß frißt.

381. (*d*) **By a Clause introduced by** wie or daß:

I observed him driving along the street.

Ich bemerkte, wie (or daß) er die Straße entlang fuhr.

382. The English elliptical construction, Conjunction + Participle, is not to be imitated in German; the Participle must be rendered by a finite verb:

While waiting for the train, I bought an evening paper.

Während ich auf den Zug wartete, kaufte ich mir eine Abendzeitung.

When next staying in London, come and see me.

Wenn Sie wieder einmal in London Aufenthalt machen, suchen Sie mich auf!

THE TENSES (das Tempus, die Tempora).

383. German has no distinctive tense-forms to mark an act or state as momentary or continuous, single or habitual.

The various meanings contained in forms such as: I work, I am working, I worked, I was working, I used to work, are differentiated in other ways.

Action in progress is expressed by the adverb eben:

Ich schreibe eben einen Brief.   I am just writing a letter.
Er aß eben zu Mittag, als ich hereintrat.
He was just lunching when I entered.

384.   **Habit** is expressed by the verb pflegen; the adverb sonst may also be used for past time:

> Er pflegt um 5 Uhr aufzustehen.   He gets up at 5.
> Sonst bekam man hier guten Wein.
> We used (formerly) to get good wine here.

385.   **Future time** is expressed not only by the Future Tense, but by wollen:

Es will (wollte) eben anfangen.   It is (was) just going to begin.

386.   Future time is also expressed, more frequently than in English, by the Present Tense, especially when intention is implied:

Also, heute gehen wir zu Ihnen, und morgen kommen Sie zu uns.
All right! To-day we are to go to your house, and to-morrow you shall come to ours.
Ich gehe ins Theater, du bleibst zu Hause.
I am going to the theatre; you must stay at home.

387.   Hence the use of the Pres. Ind. with Imperative sense:

Du bleibst da, bis ich zurückkomme!   Stay here till I return.

388.   The Future and Future-Perfect are used to express probability:

> Das kann nicht sein, du wirst dich irren.
> Impossible! you must be mistaken.
> Ich werde mich versprochen haben.
> It must have been a slip of the tongue.

389. Past Time. In conversational style, German, like French, uses the Perfect for the simple Past (Past Definite, Preterite); but where the Imperfect would be used in French, German has the Past:

Jch habe heute um 7 Uhr gefrühstückt.

I breakfasted at 7 this morning.

Was haben Sie gestern in der Stadt angefangen?

What did you find to do in town yesterday?

Haben Sie meine Freunde gesehen, als Sie in Dresden waren?

Did you see my friends when you were in Dresden?

Occasionally this tendency is reversed:

Warst du je in Deutschland? Have you ever been in Germany?

390. Present Continuous. The Present is used in German, as in French and Latin, of an act or state beginning in the past and continuing into the present:

Wie lange lernen Sie schon Deutsch?

How long have you been learning German?

Wir leben seit vier Jahren in England.

We have lived in England for four years.

Wir haben vier Jahre in England gelebt means

We lived four years in England (and now live there no longer).

The Past has a similar use:

Er wohnte seit drei Jahren in der Hochstraße.

He had been living in the High Street for three years.

GOVERNMENT OF VERBS.

391. (*a*) Verbs of incomplete predication take a Predicative Noun or Predicative Adjective in the same case as the subject. Such are sein, bleiben, werden, heißen, scheinen, and the Passives of nennen, heißen, schelten, schimpfen, preisen:

Du bist und bleibst mein bester Freund.

You are, and always will be, my best friend.

(*b*) Some verbs take two Accusatives; the first an object, the second a predicate (see § 84):

> Er nannte mich seinen Retter.　He called me his rescuer.

(*c*) The second Accusative may be preceded by als, or a prepositional phrase may be used instead (see § 86):

> Er betrachtet mich als seinen Retter.
> He looks upon me as his rescuer.
> Er hält mich für einen ehrlichen Mann.
> He thinks me an honest man.

(*d*) Lehren takes two Accusatives; also bitten and fragen, with pronoun-object (see § 84):

> Ich frage dich nur dies: wer lehrt dich Musik?
> I ask you only this: who teaches you music?

(*e*) A few verbs still govern the Genitive, but the tendency is to substitute an Accusative or prepositional phrase (see § 92):

> Gedenket derer, die euch lieben!
> Think of those who love you.

(*f*) An Accusative of the Person and Genitive of the Thing are used with anklagen and other verbs (see § 93):

> Welches Verbrechens klagen Sie mich an?
> Of what crime do you accuse me?

(*g*) A Genitive of the Thing is also used with some reflexive verbs (see § 94):

> Er befleißt sich des Tennis-spiels.
> He works hard at his tennis.

(*h*) A Dative of the Indirect Object is used with many transitive verbs, in addition to the Accusative of the Thing (see § 104):

> Ich gab ihm einen guten Rat.　I gave him good advice.

(*i*) The Dative is governed by many verbs whose English equivalents are transitive (§§ 106—109):

> Er gehorcht mir; er folgt meinem Rat.
> He obeys me; he follows my advice.

VII. ADVERBS

(bas Abverb, pl. Abverbien)

INFLECTION.

392. Adverbs do not inflect except to form the Comparative
and Superlative; and even those so inflected are nearly
all adjectives used adverbially.

393. Comparison of Adverbs:

schnell	quickly	schneller	am schnellsten
stark	strongly	stärker	„ stärksten
oft	often	öfter	„ öftesten.

394. *Irregular Comparison:*

gut	well	besser	am besten
hoch	high(ly)	höher	„ höchsten
nahe	near	näher	„ nächsten
viel	much	mehr	„ meisten
wenig	little	{ minder weniger	{ „ mindesten { „ wenigsten
balb	soon	{ eher früher	{ „ ehesten { „ frühesten
gern	gladly	lieber	„ liebsten.

395. The Superlative with am is a **Relative Superlative**,
implying a comparison with a different object or circumstance:

Dieses Gemälde gefällt mir am besten.

I like this picture best, i.e. *better* than the others.

Dieses Gemälde gefällt mir am besten, wenn ich es bei Licht
betrachte.

I like this picture best when I look at it by candle-light,
i.e. *better* than in other light.

396. The **Absolute Superlative**, which implies no comparison, has three forms:

(*a*) aufs (= auf das) beste, aufs schnellste, etc.

> Er grüßte mich aufs herzlichste.
> He greeted me most heartily, i.e. very heartily indeed.

> Sie haben diese Sonate aufs schönste gespielt.
> You have played this sonata most beautifully.

397. (*b*) bestens, schönstens, usw. Only a limited number of adverbs form this type of superlative; amongst the most useful are:

ehestens	as soon as possible	nächstens	shortly
frühestens	at the earliest	schnellstens	as quickly as possible
höchstens	at most	spätestens	at the latest
längstens	at the longest	mindestens }	at least.
meistens	mostly	wenigstens }	

> Grüßen Sie ihn schönstens (or bestens) von mir.
> Give him my kindest regards.

> Der Hut hat mindestens 30 Mark gekostet.
> That hat cost at least 30 marks.

> Das ist nicht wahr; ich wenigstens glaube es nicht.
> That is not true; I at least don't believe it.

398. (*c*) A few adverbs have superlatives in -st; the most important are:

äußerst	extremely	höchst	extremely
baldigst	as soon as possible	freundlichst	most kindly
eiligst	in great haste	gefälligst	„ „ (if you please)
ergebenst	yours faithfully (most devotedly)	gehorsamst	most obediently
		untertänigst	most humbly.

Es wäre mir äußerst unangenehm, wenn wir hier übernachten müßten.

It would be most disagreeable if we had to spend the night here.

„Danke untertänigst,“ sagte der Großvezier zum Kalifen.

"I thank you most humbly," said the Grand Vizier to the Caliph.

399. N.B. (i) best=, höchst= and some others in =st compound with participles and imply a comparison:

Die bestbewaffneten Truppen. The best-armed troops.

(ii) möglichst, as with adjectives:

Kommen Sie möglichst bald wieder!
Come back as soon as you can.

Formation of Adverbs.

400. Other Adverbs are:

(a) **A few original adverbs**, such as ab, an, auf, ein, now used mainly as prepositions or verb-prefixes; and more modern forms in =en:

außen	outside	oben	above
hinten	behind	unten	below
innen	inside	vorn	in front.

401. (b) **Old Adverbial Genitives** in -s:

abends	in the evening	nachts	by night
anders	else, otherwise	rechts	on the right
anfangs	at first	stets	always
bereits	already	stracks	straight
flugs	like a flash	tags	by day
links	on the left	teils	partly.
morgens	in the morning		

402. (c) Adjective + -lich:

gänzlich	entirely	neulich	recently
gelegentlich	occasionally	schwerlich	hardly
hoffentlich	it is to be hoped	wahrlich	truly
kürzlich	recently	wissentlich	wittingly.

403. (d) Noun or Adjective or Adverb } + -lings or -wärts:

blindlings	blindly	rücklings }	
himmelwärts	heavenwards	rückwärts }	backwards
jählings	abruptly	vorwärts	forwards.
meuchlings	treacherously		

404. (e) Adjective + Noun (usually in Genitive):

andernteils }	on the other hand	jenseits	beyond
anderseits }		keineswegs	by no means
ausnahmsweise	exceptionally	manchmal	now and again
diesseits	on this side	meistenteils	mostly
ebenfalls	likewise	merkwürdigerweise	strange to say
einigermaßen	to some extent	mittlerweile	meanwhile
einmal	once	niemals	never
glücklicherweise	fortunately	stufenweise	by degrees
größtenteils	for the most part	unglücklicherweise	unfortunately.
jemals	ever		

405. (f) Noun + Adverb; Preposition + Noun:

bergab	downhill	beizeiten	betimes, early
bergan	uphill	überhaupt	at all
feldein	across-country	übermorgen	the day after to-morrow
jahraus jahrein	year in year out	unterwegs	on the way.
stromauf	upstream		

406. (*g*) **Adverbs with Pronominal prefixes:**

Demonstrative:

hier, here; her, hither; hin, hence; heute (= hi=Tag), to-day; da, dort, there; dann, denn, then; desto, the (= by so much).

Relative and Interrogative:

wann, wenn, when; wo, where; wie, how, as.

407. (*h*) **Hier, da, wo, hin, her** + Preposition or Adverb:

hierdurch	hereby	hiermit	herewith	hiervon	hereof
dadurch	thereby	damit	therewith	davon	thereof
wodurch	whereby	womit	wherewith	wovon	whereof
hinaus} heraus}	out	hinunter} herunter}	down	hinauf} herauf}	up, etc.

408. Note that her suggests motion *towards* the point of which the speaker is thinking; hin motion *away* from it; in other words her and hin suggest *coming* and *going* respectively.

If there is a knock at the door, one says „Herein!" and the person outside kommt herein.

In sending anyone out, one says „Hinaus!" and the person geht hinaus.

Hineingehen, to go in; herauskommen, to come out.
Woher kommen Sie? (Wo kommen Sie her?)
Where do you *come from*?
Wohin gehen Sie? (Wo gehen Sie hin?)
Where are you *going to*?

409. Hervor differs from vorher, in that the former is used only of place, and means *forth*; whereas vorher is used of time:

Komme unter dem Tisch hervor! Come from under the table.
Ich hatte schon vorher gespeist. I had already dined.

ADVERBS CLASSIFIED ACCORDING TO MEANING.

410. Place.

hier	here	herab, hinab	down
da, dort	there	heran, hinan	on
daher	thence	heraus, hinaus	out
dahin	thither		
hierher	hither	wo	where
(hier)hin	hence	woher	whence
(dr)außen	outside	wohin	whither
(dr)innen	inside	irgendwo	somewhere
(dr)oben	above	nirgends	nowhere
(dr)unten	below	überall	everywhere
hierin	herein		
darin	therein	auseinander	apart
gegenüber	opposite	fern) weit)	far
zusammen	together	vorbei	past.

411. Time.

bisher	till now	noch	yet
dann und wann	now and then	noch einmal	once more
eben	just	noch nicht	not yet
endlich	at last	oft	often
erst	only	öfters	frequently
gerade	just	schon	already
gestern	yesterday	seitdem	since then
vorgestern	the day before	selten	seldom
heute	to-day [yesterday	sonst	else, formerly
heute abend	this evening	von jetzt an	henceforward
heute früh	this morning	vorher	previously
heute nacht	last night	wieder	again
immer	ever	wie lange	how long
lange	a long time	zuerst	at first
morgen	to-morrow	zuletzt	finally
nach und nach	by degrees	zunächst	first, to begin with
nicht mehr	no longer		
nicht mehr lange	not much longer	zuweilen	at times.

412. Degree, Extent, Quantity.

außerordentlich	uncommonly	ſehr	very
äußerſt	extremely	ſo	so
beinahe	nearly	ſogar	even
durchaus	absolutely	teils	partly
ebenſo...als	as...as	teilweiſe	in part
etwas	somewhat	weit	far
faſt	almost	bei weitem	by far
ganz	quite	wenig	little
ganz und gar	entirely	wenigſtens	at least
gänzlich	completely	wie (relative)	as
genug	enough	wie?	how?
kaum	scarcely	ziemlich	fairly, rather
mehr oder weniger	more or less	je...deſto ⎫	the...the...
nur	only	je...um ſo ⎭	

413. Modality.

allerdings	to be sure	nein	no
auch	also, even	nicht	not
doch	nevertheless	nicht einmal	not even
doch	(emphatic)	vielleicht	perhaps
freilich	I grant you	vielmehr	rather
gar nicht	not at all	wahrſcheinlich	probably
gewiß	certainly	wirklich ⎫	really, indeed
ja	yes	in der Tat ⎭	
ja	(emphatic)	wohl	I suppose
leider	unfortunately	zufällig	by chance.

414. Doch implies a protest, and is specially used to give an affirmative answer to a negative question :

     Hören Sie doch auf mit Ihrem Unſinn!
     Do stop your nonsense.

     Kennen Sie mich nicht? Doch, doch!
     Don't you know me? Oh, yes, I do.

$\mathfrak{Ja}$ implies that the statement is not likely to be contradicted :

> $\mathfrak{Ich}$ $\mathfrak{habe}$ $\mathfrak{es}$ $\mathfrak{dir}$ $\mathfrak{ja}$ $\mathfrak{gesagt!}$
> I told you so, you know.
>
> $\mathfrak{Das}$ $\mathfrak{ist}$ $\mathfrak{ja}$ $\mathfrak{lauter}$ $\mathfrak{Unsinn.}$
> Why, that's sheer nonsense, you know!
>
> $\mathfrak{Sie}$ $\mathfrak{kommen}$ $\mathfrak{ja}$ $\mathfrak{immer}$ $\mathfrak{spät.}$ You *always* come late.
>
> $\mathfrak{Das}$ $\mathfrak{ist}$ $\mathfrak{ja}$ $\mathfrak{mein}$ $\mathfrak{Vetter.}$ Why! That's my cousin.

$\mathfrak{Zufällig}$ is usually translated by the verb *to happen* :

> $\mathfrak{Ich}$ $\mathfrak{saß}$ $\mathfrak{zufällig}$ $\mathfrak{in}$ $\mathfrak{meiner}$ $\mathfrak{Stube.}$
> I *happened* to be sitting in my study.

VIII. PREPOSITIONS
(die Präposition)

415. Prepositions are classified in four groups, according to the cases they govern.

I. PREPOSITIONS ALWAYS GOVERNING THE ACCUSATIVE:

bis	till	ohne	without
durch	through	sonder	without
für	for	um	about
gegen	against	wider	against.

416. Bis:

Before Proper Names, Numerals, Adverbs:

bis Oftern	till Easter	bis Berlin	as far as Berlin
drei bis vier Tage	3 or 4 days	bis heute	till to-day;

or followed by a Preposition:

bis an die Ohren	up to the ears
bis auf weiteres	till further notice
bis auf den Grund	down to the ground
alle bis auf zwei	all save two.

Cf. the use of mitten: mitten im Winter, in midwinter.

417. Durch:

(a) Of Place:

Er fuhr durch das Dorf.   He drove through the village.

(b) Of Time:

Wir wachten durch die Nacht⟩   We kept watch through-
Wir wachten die Nacht durch⟨.   out the night.

(c) Of Means:

Durch solche Taten wurde er berühmt.
By such means did he become famous.

418. Für:

(a) For the sake of, for the advantage of:

Mit Gott für König und Vaterland.

With God for King and country.

Das habe ich für Sie gekauft.

I have bought that for you.

(b) In exchange for, as the equivalent of:

Ich habe es für zwei Mark {gekauft. I bought it for 2 marks.
{verkauft. I sold it for 2 marks.

Ich halte ihn für einen ehrlichen Mann.

I take him to be an honest man.

(c) Considering:

Für seine Jahre ist er sehr unerfahren.

He is very inexperienced for his age.

Note: Ich kann nichts dafür.   I cannot help it.

Es ist teuer, aber dafür ist es sehr gut.

It is dear, but it is very good (to compensate).

419. Gegen:

(a) Of Direction:

Gegen den Strom schwimmen.   To swim upstream.

Er blickte gegen (or gen) Himmel.

He looked towards the sky.

(b) Opposition:

Gegen die Franzosen kämpfen. To fight against the French.

Gegen alle Erwartungen.   Contrary to expectation.

Haben Sie etwas dagegen?   Have you any objection?

(c) Exchange:

Wir verkaufen nur gegen bar Geld.   We sell only for cash.

(d) Comparison:

Gegen Sie bin ich ganz klein.

Compared to you I am quite short.

(*e*) Figuratively, of the direction of a sentiment (French *envers*):

Er ist gegen uns freundlich gesinnt.

He is well disposed towards us.

(*f*) Approximation:

Gegen hundert Mann.   About a hundred men.

Gegen Abend; gegen vier Uhr.

Towards evening; about four o'clock.

420. Ohne:

Ohne Fleiß kein Preis.   No work, no prize.

Ohne das Buch gelesen zu haben.

Without having read the book.

Ohne weiteres; ohnehin.   Without more ado; all the same.

421. Sonder:

Only in the expressions:

Sonder Zahl; sondergleichen.   Without number; peerless.

422. Um:

(*a*) Of Place:

Wir saßen um das Feuer.   We sat round the fire.

Wir gingen um die Stadt (herum).

We walked round the town, i.e. made a circuit around it.

But Wir gingen in der Stadt umher.

We walked round the town, i.e. up and down in it.

(*b*) Of the object for which one fights, strives, asks:

Um etwas kämpfen, streiten, bitten, ringen, sich kümmern.

Kümmern Sie sich um Ihre eignen Sachen!

Mind your own business.

(*c*) Of the price of a purchase or exchange:

Um jeden Preis; um die Welt nicht.

At any price; not for all the world.

Um nichts; umsonst.   For nothing.

Auge um Auge, Zahn um Zahn.   An eye for an eye, etc.

Compare Um des Himmels willen.   For Heaven's sake.

(*d*) Of Time, sometimes approximately, sometimes exactly:

Um Mitternacht; um halb brei.

About midnight; at half-past two.

(*e*) Measure of Difference:

Er ift um einen ganzen Kopf größer als bu.

He is a whole head taller than you.

Um bie Hälfte mehr. Half as much again.

Um fo mehr, all the more ; um ein Haar, all but.

(*f*) Es ift um uns gefchehen. It is all up with us.

Er ift ums Leben gekommen. He has lost his life.

Er hat mich um mein Gelb gebracht.

He has robbed me of my money.

423. Wiber:

Always expresses resistance or opposition, unlike gegen, which may express mere direction :

Wiber den Strom fchwimmen; wiber den Feind kämpfen.

Das ift wiber meinen Befehl. That is against my orders.

Das Für und Wiber. The pros and cons.

II. PREPOSITIONS GOVERNING THE ACCUSATIVE OR DATIVE.

424. An, auf, hinter, in, neben, über, unter, vor, zwifchen.

In answer to the question Wo? these prepositions take the Dative; in answer to the question Wohin? they take the Accusative.

When used figuratively, an and in more frequently take the Dative, and auf and über the Accusative.

425. **An** denotes physical contact or proximity, and therefore must be distinguished from auf, which denotes superposition. Thus Wir fiten am Tifch means We sit at table; Wir sitzen auf dem Tisch, we sit on the table. When we dress, wir ziehen unsre Kleider an; but wir setzen den Hut auf. Derivatively, it is used of the point of intellectual contact, and so of almost any logical connection between a verb of thinking or feeling and its noun.

(*a*) Place:

Das Gemälde hängt an der Wand.
The picture hangs on the wall.
Er trägt einen Ring am Finger.
He wears a ring on his finger.
Ich packte ihn am Rock.   I seized him by the coat.
Frankfurt am Main.   Frankfort on the Main.
Am Wege.   By the wayside.

Note: Am Boden.   On the ground.   Also auf dem Boden.

(*b*) Time, like English *on*, to denote *the day* on which something happened:

Am ersten Juli.   On the 1st of July.
An einem Sonntage.   On a Sunday.
An jenem Abend.   On that evening.

(*c*) Point of intellectual contact:

Ich erkenne ihn an seinen Schultern.
I know him by his shoulders.
Ich sehe es an der Handschrift.
I see it by the handwriting.

(*d*) In respect of:

Reich an Freunden; arm an Gelde.
Rich in friends; poor in purse.
Es fehlt ihm an Verstand.   He lacks intelligence.
Sie leidet an den Nerven.   She suffers from nerves.
Er ist an seiner Ehre gekränkt.
He suffers injury touching his honour; his honour is impugned.

(*e*) With verbs of feeling, etc. :

An etwas Luſt haben, Gefallen finden.
To take delight in a thing.

Sich an etwas freuen.   To be glad of…

Sich an einem rächen.   To take vengeance on…

An etwas zweifeln, verzweifeln.   To doubt of, despair of…

Er hat an mir redlich gehandelt.   He has dealt fairly by me.

(*f*) With the Accusative, to denote the direction of
thought, etc.:

An etwas glauben, denken, ſich erinnern, ſich gewöhnen.
To believe in, think of, remember, accustom oneself to
something.

Ich ſchreibe an meinen Bruder.
I am writing to my brother.

426. Auf, *upon* :

(*a*) Place:

Auf dem Berge, on the hill. Auf dem Dache, on the roof.
Sich auf den Weg machen, to start; compare *se mettre
en route*.

(*b*) At or to an elevated place, and so of most public
buildings, etc. :

Auf der Burg; auf dem Schloß; auf der Poſt; auf der
Schule; auf der Univerſität; auf dem Rathaus; auf dem
Markt; auf dem Bahnhof.

(*c*) Of unenclosed places:

Auf dem Meere; auf der Erde; auf dem Felde (German
fields being unfenced); auf der Welt; auf der Straße;
auf dem Lande.

(*d*) To express Aim, Object, Purpose, etc. :

Auf etwas zielen. To aim at. Auf etwas hören. To listen to.

Auf etwas hoffen, achten, sich vorbereiten, warten, sinnen, sich besinnen, sich freuen.

To hope for, pay heed to, prepare for, wait for, devise, recollect, look forward to something.

Besinne dich auf das dumme Wort.

Try to remember the silly word.

(e) Of Time, always with Accusative; expresses intention:

Er hat das Haus auf drei Jahre gemietet.

He has taken the house for three years.

Ich reise auf 3 Monate nach Frankreich.

I am going to France for three months.

Auf Wiedersehen!   Au revoir.

(f) Note:

Stolz, neidisch, eifersüchtig auf.   Proud, envious, jealous of.

Auf diese Weise.   In this way.   Auf deutsch.   In German.

Auf der Stelle.   On the spot.   Auf der Jagd.   Hunting.

Auf die Jagd gehen.   To go hunting.

Auf seine Frage.   In reply to his question.

Auf alle Fälle. At all events. Auf Ihren Rat. On your advice.

427. Hinter, *behind*:

Er stand hinter dem Baume.   He stood behind the tree.

Er stellte sich hinter den Baum.

He placed himself behind the tree.

Er kam hinter dem Baume hervor.

He came from behind the tree.

428. In has many uses, which present little difficulty, as most of them correspond with the English usage.

(a) Place:

Er ging in die Stadt; er blieb in der Stadt.

Ich habe mir in den Finger geschnitten.

I have cut my finger.

Er klatſchte in die Hände.   He clapped his hands.

In die Schule, in die Kirche, ins Konzert, ins Theater gehen.
To go to school, to church, to the concert, to the theatre.

In der Schule, in der Kirche, im Konzert, im Theater ſein.
To be at school, at church, at the concert, at the play.

In einiger Entfernung.   At some distance.

(*b*) Time:

Im Jahre 1927; im Sommer; im September; in dieſem
Augenblick, at this moment; in einem Augenblick; in einer
Stunde (= French, *en une heure* or *dans une heure*).

(*c*) Of Manner, Circumstance:

Im Kriege und im Frieden.   At war and at peace.

In Freiheit. At liberty.   In Verlegenheit. At a loss.

In hohem Grade, im höchſten Grade.
To a high degree, extremely.

Im Schritt, im Trabe, im Galopp, im vollen Galopp.
At walking pace, at a trot, at a gallop, at full gallop.

Im Gegenteil.   On the contrary.

In der Abſicht.   With the intention.

Im Durchſchnitt.   On the average.

429. Neben, *beside*:

(*a*) Place:

Er ſaß neben mir.   He sat beside me.

Er ſetzte ſich neben mich.   He sat down beside me.

(*b*) = Außer, nebſt:

Neben anderen Dingen.   Amongst other things.

(*c*) 'Compared with'; cf. gegen.

430. Über, *over*:

(*a*) Place:

Der Vogel ſchwebt über dem See; er fliegt über den See.
The bird hovers over the lake; it flies over the lake.

With the Acc. the sense of über is 'across, from one side to the other'; it therefore definitely indicates a change of place, and answers the question „Wohin?" With the Dat., though there is motion, the scene of the motion is not altered. In „Er flog über dem See" there is motion, but the scene of it is still the lake; whereas in „Er flog über den See" the scene changes from one side of the lake to the other.

So, über einen Fluß setzen.   To cross a river.
Er ist über alle Berge.
He is far away, lit. he has crossed the hills.

Hence the sense of *via*, as in
Er fuhr über München nach Wien.
He travelled *via* Munich to Vienna.

(*b*) Occupation:
Er saß über seinen Büchern. He sat poring over his books.

And with the idea of Cause:
Über dem Spiel vergaßen wir unsre Geschäfte.
We were so engrossed in our game that we forgot our business.

(*c*) Over, above, or beyond a measure, with Acc.:
Über die Maßen, über alle Maßen.
Beyond measure, immoderately.
Über zwanzig Jahre.   More than 20 years.
Über alle Erwartungen.   Beyond all expectation.

(*d*) Superiority, with Acc.:
Er triumphierte über alle seine Feinde.
He triumphed over all his enemies.
Wir haben einen Vorteil über ihn.
We have an advantage over him.
Es geht nichts übers Leder.
There's nothing like leather.

(e) Of Time, with Acc.:

> Heute über acht Tage.   This day week.
> Über kurz oder lang.   Sooner or later.

(f) Concerning, to express the subject of thought, feeling or speech, with Acc.:

> Wir haben über Ihren Freund nachgedacht.
> We have been thinking about your friend.
> Über etwas lachen, trauern, sich freuen, sprechen, schreiben.
> To laugh about (at), mourn for, rejoice at, talk about, write about something.

431. **Unter**, the opposite of über:

(a) Of Place: beneath, below:

> Er kroch unter den Tisch; er lag unter dem Tisch.
> Er kroch unter dem Tisch hervor.
> He crept out from under the table.
> Das Thermometer steht unter Null.
> The thermometer is below zero.

(b) Of Measure: below, less than:

> Er ist unter 40 Jahren.   He is under 40.
> Dieses Pferd ist unter tausend Mark nicht zu haben.
> This horse cannot be bought for less than 1000 marks.

(c) Inferiority:

> Er hat 50 Mann unter sich.   He has 50 men under him.
> Dieser Aufsatz ist unter aller Kritik.
> This essay is execrable.
> Das Pfund Sterling steht unter Pari.
> The £ sterling is below par.

(d) Among:

> Ich saß unter den Zuschauern.   I sat among the spectators.
> Unter anderm.   Amongst other things.
> Der größte unter uns.   The tallest of us.

(*e*) Of Circumstances:

Unter biefen Umftänben.   In the circumstances.

Unter bem Donner ber Kanonen.

Amidst the thunder of the guns.

Unter biefer Bebingung.   On this condition.

Unter ber Regierung bes großen Friebrich.

In the reign of Frederick the Great.

432. **Vor,** *before*:

(*a*) Of Place: before, in the presence of:

Er ftanb vor bem Richter.   He stood before the judge.

Man fchleppte ihn vor ben Richter.

He was dragged before the judge.

Ich fezte ihn vor bie Tür.   I turned him out of the room.

(*b*) Of the object whose presence produces emotion, and
so of Cause, more widely:

Er zitterte vor mir.   He trembled before me.

Ich habe Angft vor ihm.   I am afraid of him.

Ich fürchte mich, fchäme mich, fcheue mich vor ihm.

Ich zittre vor Kälte, fterbe vor Durft, fpringe vor Freube.

I am trembling with cold, dying of thirst, leaping for joy.

(*c*) Before, i.e. from, a pursuer:

Er flieht vor bem Feinbe.   He flees from the enemy.

Schützen Sie mich vor bem Winbe!

Shield me from the wind.

Wer fichert mich vor meinen Feinben?

Who will protect me from my enemies?

So also:

Ich warne bich vor ihm.   I warn you against him.

Du verbirgft es vor mir.   You are hiding it from me.

(*d*) Of Time:

Vor acht Uhr, vor Oftern.   Before 8 o'clock, before Easter.

Vor einem Monat, vor kurzem.   A month ago, recently.

433. **Zwischen**:

Er saß zwischen mir und dir. He sat between me and you.
Er setzte sich zwischen mich und dich.
He sat down between me and you.
Zwischen fünf und sechs Uhr.
Between four and five o'clock.

III. PREPOSITIONS GOVERNING THE DATIVE.

434. Aus, bei, mit, nach, von, zu;
aus, binnen, nebst, samt, seit, trotz;
entgegen, gegenüber, gemäß, zufolge, zuwider, dank.

435. **Aus**, the opposite of in:

(a) From, out of an enclosed space:
Er zog ein Messer aus seiner Tasche.
He drew a knife from his pocket.

(b) To express Origin:
Er ist aus Italien gebürtig. He is a native of Italy.
Der Herr aus Italien. The gentleman from Italy.
Ein Märchen aus alten Zeiten. A tale of olden days.

(c) Material, Composition:
Ein Bild aus Holz schnitzen. To carve a figure in wood.
Ein Auto besteht aus Gestell und Karosserie.
A car consists of chassis and body.
Aus nichts wird nichts. Ex nihilo nihil fit.
Was ist aus ihm geworden? What has become of him?

(d) The Source of one's knowledge; and so the Motive
of an act:
Aus Erfahrung; aus der Geschichte.
From experience; from history.
Aus Dankbarkeit, Freundlichkeit, Liebe, Eifersucht handeln.
To act from gratitude, kindness, love, jealousy.

436. Bei, *beside*:

    (*a*) Of Place, denotes Proximity:

        Ich saß nahe bei ihm.   I sat close by him.

        Die Schlacht bei Jena.   The battle of Jena.

        Bei Tisch; bei der Arbeit.   At table; at work.

    Hence Occupation:

        Beim Spiele; beim Unterricht.   At play; at lessons.

    (*b*) Of closer contact, on the person, in the house or
        country of:

        Hast du kein Geld bei dir?   Have you no money on you?

        Bei meinem Onkel; bei uns.   At my uncle's; at our house.

        Bei Müllers; bei uns zu Lande.

        At the Müllers'; in our country.

    (*c*) Of Time or Circumstances:

        Bei Tage; bei Nacht.   By day; by night.

        Bei günstigem Wetter.   In favourable weather.

        Bei dieser Gelegenheit.   On this occasion.

        Er ist bei Gelde; bei guter Gesundheit.

        He is in funds, in good health.

        Bei Tagesanbruch; bei einbrechender Nacht.

        At daybreak; at nightfall.

        Bei meiner Ankunft.   On my arrival.

    Note also:

        Bei weitem.   By far.

        Bei meiner Ehre!   Upon my honour.

437. Mit expresses conjunction or association. Most of its
derivative uses correspond to those of the English *with*.

    (*a*) Physical Association:

        Ich bin mit meinem Bruder gefahren.

        I travelled with my brother.

        Ich habe mich mit ihm geschlagen.   I fought with him.

        Ein Beefsteak mit Bratkartoffeln.

        Beefsteak with fried potatoes.

(*b*) Logical Association, and so Description :

Mit Recht; mit Fleiß.   With justice; with diligence.

Was ist's mit ihm?   What is the matter with him ?

Mit etwas zufrieden.   Satisfied with a thing.

Er ist mit seiner Arbeit fertig.   He has finished his work.

Heraus damit!   Out with it !

Der Mann mit der eisernen Maske.

The man with the iron mask.

Ein Junge mit schmutzigen Händen.   A boy with dirty hands.

(*c*) Instrumentality or Means :

Mit der Post; mit der Bahn.   By post; by train.

Ich kann mit dieser Feder nicht schreiben.

I can't write with this pen.

(*d*) Time :

Mit der Zeit; mit zwanzig Jahren.

In course of time; at the age of twenty.

Mit dem Glockenschlage zwölf.   On the stroke of twelve.

438. Nach, akin to nahe, *nigh*, expresses :

(*a*) The Direction of Movement with names of Places :

Nach Spanien; nach London; nach Amerika.

To Spain, London, America.

(But Gehen Sie zu meinem Onkel!   Go to my uncle !)

Nach Süden; nach allen Richtungen.

Southward; in all directions.

(*b*) The Direction of Effort :

Nach einem Ziele schießen.   To shoot at a mark.

Er griff nach seiner Pistole.   He clutched at his pistol.

Er schickte nach dem Arzt.   He sent for the doctor.

After sich sehnen, to yearn, streben, strive, forschen, enquire, fragen, ask, etc.

(*c*) Of Time, *after* :

Gleich nach meiner Ankunft.   Immediately after my arrival.

Nach Ihnen, bitte!   After you, please.

But Laufen Sie ihm nach!   Run after him !

(*d*) In accordance with; cf. French *d'après*:

Ich urteile nach dem Schein. I judge by appearances.

Nach meinem Geschmack; nach Belieben.

To my taste; as you please.

Meiner Meinung nach; allem Anschein nach.

In my opinion; to all appearance.

Note: Nach Wein schmecken; nach Tabak riechen.

To taste of wine, smell of tobacco.

439. **Von** indicates the Point of Departure.

(*a*) Of Place: very like the English *from*, but to be carefully distinguished from aus, which should be used whenever the sense is 'out of':

Er kommt von Paris.

But Er ist aus Paris aufs Land gekommen.

Er reiste von Paris nach Berlin.

Er nahm den Hut vom Kopfe.

He took his hat from off his head.

Von Ort zu Ort; von Haus zu Haus.

From place to place; from house to house.

(*b*) Separation:

Befreie mich von diesen Banden!

Free me from these bonds!

After trennen, sondern, separate; erlösen, deliver; retten, rescue; heilen, heal, etc.

(*c*) Origin, Source:

Ein Brief von dem König. A letter from the King.

Wasser von der Quelle. Water from the spring.

Der Kaufmann von Venedig. The Merchant of Venice.

Hence as a title of nobility: Rudolf von Habsburg.

(*d*) Description:

Ein Mann von Ehre, von Stand.

A man of honour; of rank.

Ein Greis von achtzig Jahren. An old man of eighty.

Schurke von einem Wirt! Rogue of a landlord!

(*e*) Of Time:

Von Zeit zu Zeit; von jetzt an.

From time to time; henceforth.

Von Jugend auf; von alters her.

From (my) youth up; from time immemorial.

(*f*) Concerning, like über:

After denken, meinen, glauben, hören, erzählen, sprechen, etc.

Wir sprachen von der Erziehung. We talked of education.

N.B. Ein Haus, von dem ich weiß, daß es zu klein ist.

A house which I know to be too small.

(*g*) To express the Agent after a Passive Verb:

Wir wurden von dem Feinde angeschossen.

We were fired at by the enemy.

Also of inanimate agents:

Der Baum wurde vom Winde umgerissen.

The tree was blown down by the wind.

(*h*) As a substitute for the Genitive; see § 101.

440. **Zu** directs attention to a point, differing from nach, which expresses mere direction, an, which means contact along a line, auf, used of superposition, and in, of enclosure.

(*a*) Of Place:

(i) Rest: sometimes with proper names of towns, but in this sense in is more frequent:

Der Dom zu Köln. The cathedral at Cologne.

In a few set phrases:

Zu Hause; (mir) zur Seite. At home; at (my) side.

Zum goldnen Löwen. At the sign of the Golden Lion.

(ii) Motion: with names of persons, nach being used with place-names:

Führet mich zu eurem Hauptmann!

Lead me to your captain.

In set phrases:

> Zu Grunde gehen; zu Boden fallen.
> To perish; fall to the ground.
> Zu Tisch gehen; zu Bett gehen. To go to dinner, to bed.
> Von Ort zu Ort; von Haus zu Haus.
> From place to place; from house to house.

(*b*) Of Time at which, or to which:

> Zu Weihnachten; zu Michaelis, Ostern, Pfingsten.
> At Christmas; at Michaelmas, Easter, Whitsun.
> Zur rechten Zeit; zu Mittag essen.
> At the right time; to dine.
> Von Zeit zu Zeit; von Tag zu Tag.
> From time to time; from day to day.

(*c*) Of Direction or Tendency:

> Das gereicht Ihnen zur Ehre. That is to your credit.
> Es ist zum Totlachen.
> It is enough to make you die of laughter.
> Aus Neigung (Liebe) zu ihm.
> From affection for him, love of him.

Especially before Infinitives, after wünschen, zwingen, bereit sein, hoffen, bewegen, etc.; and as the equivalent of the Latin supine in *u*, or Gerundive:

> Ich bin bereit zu sterben. I am prepared to die.
> Er ist schwer zu befriedigen. He is hard to please.
> Es ist nicht auszuhalten.
> It is not to be endured, intolerable.

See § 361.

(*d*) Of Purpose:

> Ich tue es dir zu Ehren (Gefallen).
> I do it in your honour, for your pleasure.
> Wasser zum Trinken. Drinking-water.
> Sich zum Kriege rüsten. To prepare for war.

Especially in um zu with Infinitive:

> Man muß essen, um zu leben. One must eat to live.

(*e*) Of Result, especially after verbs of appointing, electing:

Zum Kaiser wählen; zum König krönen.

To elect emperor, crown king.

Zum Minister ernennen.   To appoint as minister.

Zum Hauptmann befördern.   To promote captain.

Er hat zu meiner Zufriedenheit gearbeitet.

He has worked to my satisfaction.

(*f*) Note also:

Eine Marke zu 50 Pfennig.   A 50-pfennig stamp.

Er kam zur Türe herein.   He came in by the door.

Er warf es zum Fenster hinaus.

He threw it out of the window.

Zu Fuß; zu Pferd; zu Land; zu Wasser.

On foot; on horse-back; by land; by water.

Zum Glück; zum Beispiel.   Fortunately, for instance.

Zum Teil; zu Tausenden.   Partly, by the thousand.

441. Zu in compounds often forms a kind of *postposition*:

Dir zu Ehren.   In your honour.

Dir zuliebe; dir zu Gefallen.   To please you.

Der Welt zum Trotze.   In spite of all the world.

Dieses Pferd ist mir zuteil geworden.

This horse has fallen to my lot.

Diesem Gesetz zufolge. ⎱
or Zufolge dieses Gesetzes. ⎰ In accordance with this law.

or Den neuesten Nachrichten zufolge. ⎱ According to the
   Zufolge der neuesten Nachrichten. ⎰   latest news.

Dem Gesetz zuwider.   Contrary to the law.

442. Außer, *out of,* is no longer used of place (außerhalb).

(*a*) Of Condition:

Außer Gefahr; außer Atem.

Out of danger; out of breath.

Ein Major außer Dienst (a. D.).   A retired major.

Er ist außer sich.   He is beside himself.

(*b*) *Except, besides*:

Außer mir ist keiner geblieben. None but myself remained.

443. **Binnen**, *within*: of Time only:

Binnen acht Tagen kam er zurück.
Within a week he returned.

444. **Nebst, samt**, *together with*. Samt is stronger than nebst, and implies that the two things would not normally be taken together:

Ein Briefbogen nebst Couvert.
A sheet of note-paper and an envelope.
Sie aß den Käse samt der Rinde. Rind and all.

445. **Seit**, *since*:

Seit dem Kriege; seit gestern.
Since the war; since yesterday.

Note: Seit wann lernen Sie Deutsch?
How long have you been learning German?

See § 390.

446. **Trotz**, *in spite of*: also governs the Gen.:

Trotz dem schlechten Wetter. In spite of the bad weather.
Trotzdem; trotz alledem. Nevertheless; for all that.

447. **Entgegen**, *towards*, *in the contrary direction*; usually after its noun:

Dem Strom entgegen. Up stream.
Meinen Wünschen entgegen. Against my wishes.
Er kam mir entgegen. He came to meet me.
Er kam meinen Wünschen entgegen. He met my wishes.

448. **Gegenüber**, *opposite*, generally placed after its noun:

Mir gegenüber saß eine alte Dame.
Opposite me sat an old lady.

449. **Gemäß**, *according to*:

    Ihrer Bitte gemäß. In compliance with your request.

    Er lebt nicht der Natur gemäß.

    He does not live a natural life.

    Sie leben ihrem Stande gemäß.

    They live up to their position.

(The adverbs naturgemäß, standesgemäß, could have been used to express the same meaning.)

450. **Zufolge**, *according to*; **zuwider**, *contrary to*: see § 441.

451. **Dank**, *thanks to*:

    Dank seinem Fleiße wurde er versetzt.

    Thanks to his industry he was promoted.

452. IV. PREPOSITIONS GOVERNING THE GENITIVE ARE MAINLY DERIVED FROM NOUNS:

anstatt, statt, instead of

diesseit(s), jenseit(s), on this side of, beyond

entlang, längs, along

halb, halber, halben, for the sake of

außerhalb, outside

innerhalb, inside

oberhalb, above

unterhalb, below

kraft, by virtue of

laut, according to

mittels, vermittels }

mittelst, vermittelst } by means of

trotz (also with dat.), in spite of

um...willen, for the sake of

vermöge, by dint of

wegen, during.

453. **Anstatt**:

    Ich komme (an)statt meines Bruders. } I come instead of

        or an meines Bruders Statt. }   my brother.

    (An)statt zu wachen, schlief er ein.

    Instead of watching, he fell asleep.

454. **Diesseit**:

    Diesseit des Flusses; jenseit des Flusses.

    This side of the river; beyond the river.

455. Entlang:

Entlang (or längs) der Front.   Along the line.

Also: Er ritt die Front entlang.   He rode along the front.

456. Halb, etc.:

Ich verzeihe ihm seiner Jugend halber.

I forgive him for the sake of his youth.

Ich bleibe des schlechten Wetters halber zu Hause.

On account of the bad weather I am staying at home.

Meinethalben mag er kommen.

He may come, as far as I am concerned.

Wir wohnen $\begin{Bmatrix} \text{außerhalb} \\ \text{innerhalb} \end{Bmatrix}$ der Stadt.

We live $\begin{Bmatrix} \text{outside} \\ \text{inside} \end{Bmatrix}$ the town.

Innerhalb eines Jahres wird er zurückkommen.

Within a year he will return.

Die Mühle steht $\begin{Bmatrix} \text{oberhalb} \\ \text{unterhalb} \end{Bmatrix}$ der Brücke.

The mill is $\begin{Bmatrix} \text{above} \\ \text{below} \end{Bmatrix}$ the bridge.

457. Kraft:

Kraft meines Amtes verhafte ich Sie.

In virtue of my office, I arrest you.

458. Laut:

Laut dieser Urkunde sind (wären) Sie der Erbe.

According to this document you are the heir.

459. Mittels, etc.:

Mittels(t) eines Kahnes setzten wir über den Rhein.

By means of a boat, we crossed the Rhine.

460. Trotz:

Trotz des schlechten Wetters bin ich da.

In spite of the bad weather, here I am.

461. Um...willen:

Um des Friedens willen gab ich nach.
For the sake of peace I yielded.
Um's (Um des) Himmels willen. For Heaven's sake.

462. Vermöge:

Vermöge ungeheurer Anstrengungen ist es ihm gelungen.
By dint of desperate efforts he succeeded.

463. Während, *during*, is the present participle of the verb
während, *to last*; the adverbial genitive während des Krieges
became während des Krieges, during the war.

464. Wegen:

Wegen des schlechten Wetters.} On account of the bad
or Des schlechten Wetters wegen.} weather.
Ich habe ihn wegen dieses guten Aufsatzes gelobt.
I have praised him for this good essay.
Er wurde wegen seines Geldes ermordet.
He was murdered for (the sake of) his money.
Ich komme wegen des Mietgeldes.
I have come about the rent.
Meinetwegen. For all I care.

465. Numerous adverbs are followed by the genitive and
may be classified as prepositions. They are used less
in the spoken language than in the language of com-
merce, officialdom and journalism, to which they impart
a savour of precision and formality. Such are:

anläßlich, apropos of
ausschließlich, excluding
einschließlich, including
angesichts, in consideration of
betreffs, with reference to
bezüglich, with regard to
hinsichtlich, respecting
seitens, on the part of
unfern, unweit, not far from
ungeachtet, notwithstanding
zwecks, for the purpose of.

MNEMONICS.

466. 1. Prepositions with Acc. only:

> Cum burch, für, gegen, um, et ohne
> Accusativum semper pone.

467. 2. Prepositions with Acc. or Dat.:

> Än, auf, hinter, in and nében,
> über, unter, zwischen, vor.

468. 3. Prepositions with Dat. only:

> Schreibt aús, bei, mít, nach, seít, von, zú,
> Nebst, sámt, gemáß, zuwíder,
> Entgégen, binnen, aúßer, dánk,
> Stets mit dem Dativ nieder.

469. 4. Prepositions with Gen. only:

> Unweit, mittelst, kraft und während,
> Laut, vermöge, ungeachtet,
> Oberhalb und unterhalb,
> Innerhalb und außerhalb,
> Diesseit, jenseit, halben, wegen,
> Statt, auch längs, zufolge, trotz.

IX. CONJUNCTIONS
(die Konjunktion)

470. Conjunctions are classified as (i) Co-ordinative, (ii) Adverbial and (iii) Subordinative.

CO-ORDINATIVE CONJUNCTIONS.

471.

und, and	denn, nämlich, for
oder, or	aber, allein, sondern, but

These have no effect on the order of words in the clause or sentence which they introduce:

Ich esse, und mein Bruder hungert.
I eat and my brother is starving.
Sie sind Herr Müller, oder ich irre mich.
You are Herr M., or I am mistaken.

472. **Aber** may either begin its clause or be inserted later, in parenthesis:

Heute regnet es, morgen aber kommt schönes Wetter.
It is raining to-day, but fine weather is coming to-morrow.

Allein always comes first:

Zwar sind sie an das Beste nicht gewöhnt,
Allein sie haben schrecklich viel gelesen.
True, they are not accustomed to the best, but they have read a dreadful number of books.

Sondern is used only after a negative, and instead of contradicting or limiting the previous sentence, re-states it in affirmative form:

Er ist nicht reich, sondern arm. He is not rich but poor.
Er ist nicht nur dumm, sondern auch faul.
He is not only stupid, but also lazy.

These sentences can be turned by stating the second part first:

> He is poor, and not rich.   He is both lazy and stupid.

It will be observed that in English we now require the conjunction *and*. This test will serve to distinguish the sentences requiring ſonbern from those requiring aber, such as:

> Herr X. wirb M. 100 beitragen; er iſt nicht reich, aber er iſt ſehr freigebig.
>
> Herr X. will subscribe 100 marks; he is not rich, *but* he is very generous.

If we reverse this sentence, we shall turn *he is not rich* into a concessive clause:

> He is very generous, *though* he is not rich.

Compare also the example given with allein.

473. **Nor.** German has no equivalent to the English *nor*. Usually it can be expressed by auch nicht:

> I don't know the man, nor do I wish to make his acquaintance.
>
> Ich kenne ben Mann nicht, auch habe ich keine Luſt, ihn kennen ʒu lernen.
>
> I am not tired.—Nor I. Ich bin nicht mübe.—Ich auch nicht.

Neither...nor, weber...noch:

> Weber er, noch ſie iſt kranf. Neither he nor she is ill.

ADVERBIAL CONJUNCTIONS.

474. This name is applied to a large number of adverbs which are used to show the logical connection between sentences. They affect the order of words as other adverbs would, that is to say, when they come first, the verb will precede the subject. The most useful are:

alſo, therefore	jeboch, nevertheless
ba, there, then	natürlich, of course
bann, then	nun, now

barauf, thereupon	ſo, so, thus
benn, then	ſonſt, else
bennoch, however	trotzbem, nevertheless
beßhalb, therefore	übrigens, moreover, incidentally
boch, but	wohl, presumably
freilich, to be sure	zwar } true, I grant you, to
gleichfalls, likewise	allerbings } be sure.

475. **Alſo**: particularly useful in conversation. It may stand first, followed by a comma, in which case it does not cause inversion; or it may be placed in parenthesis:

Alſo, Sie kommen morgen!
Alſo, morgen kommen Sie! } Very well, then, you are coming to-morrow.

Morgen alſo kommen Sie! You are coming to-morrow, then.

476. **Da**: not to be confused with the subordinative conjunction ba:

Im Jahre 1914 ſtubierte ich in Heibelberg, ba brach ber Krieg aus.

In 1914 I was studying in Heidelberg, *when* the War broke out. See § 479.

477. **Denn**: to be distinguished from benn above. Always parenthetic:

Wo iſt er benn? Where *can* he be?

Wollt ihr benn ewig leben? Do you want to live *for ever*?

Das iſt benn boch Beweis genug.

After all, that is sufficient proof.

478. **Nun**: generally inferential, suggesting some logical connection between the past and the present. With jetzt there is no such connection implied:

Als nun ber Abenb kam.... Now, when evening came,....

Nun ging jeber ſeinen Weg. So each went his way.

Nun trug es ſich einmal zu, baß....

Now it happened one day....

But Es iſt jetzt (or nun) halb zwei. It is now half-past one.

479. 𝔖o: besides its ordinary meaning *thus*, ſo is used to introduce the main sentence after a subordinate clause:

> Wenn Sie Geld haben, ſo können Sie mir was borgen.
> If you have any money, you can lend me some.

It is not used to connect the sentences of a narrative; in popular language this function is performed by da:

> Da ſprach der alte König.　So the old king said.
> Da antwortete der treue Johannes.
> So Faithful John answered.

Or a subordinate clause may be formed:

> He had no money, so he had to work.
> Da er kein Geld hatte, ſo mußte er arbeiten.

SUBORDINATIVE CONJUNCTIONS.

480. The most important are:

als, as, when, than	obgleich, obſchon ⎫
als ob, als wenn, as if	obwohl　　　　　⎭ though
bis, till	ſobald, as soon as
da, as	ſolange, as long as
damit, in order that	ſo oft, as often as
daß, that	während, while
ehe, bevor, before	weil, because
falls, in case	wenn, if
indem, while	wenn auch ⎫
je...deſto, the...the	wenn gleich ⎬ though, even if
je nachdem, according as	wenn ſchon ⎪
nachdem, after	und wenn ⎭
nun, now that	wie, as
ob, whether	wo, where.

All these introduce subordinate clauses and require the verb to be placed at the end of the clause.

481. Wenn, wann, als:

Wenn (i) *if*; (ii) *when*, referring to present or future time;
(iii) *whenever*, *when*, referring to a repeated occurrence
in past time.

Wann always interrogative.

Als (i) *as*, in comparison; (ii) *when*, of a single occurrence
or state in the past.

Ich werde das Buch heute lesen, wenn ich Zeit habe.
I will read the book to-day, if I have time.
Ich werde es ihm sagen, wenn ich ihn sehe.
I will tell him when I see him.
Vorigen Sommer spielten wir Bridge, wenn es regnete.
Last summer we used to play bridge when it rained.
Es regnete, als wir in Dover ankamen.
It was raining when we arrived in Dover.
Als ich noch jung war, ging ich oft ins Theater.
When I was young, I often went to the theatre.
Ich weiß nicht, wann er gefrühstückt hat.
I don't know when he breakfasted.

482. Bis:

Warten Sie, bis er kommt.   Wait till he comes.
Wir wollten warten, bis er käme.
We wanted to wait till he should come.

483. Da:

Da Sie nun hier sind, so können Sie bleiben.
As you are here, you may stay.

484. Damit:

Arbeite fleißig, damit du versetzt wirst.
Work hard, in order that you may be promoted.

See §§ 339, 579.

485. Daß:

  (i) Purpose = damit.

  (ii) Consequence:

  Er sprach so leise, daß ich kein Wort vernehmen konnte.
  He spoke so softly that I could not hear a word.

  (iii) Noun-Clause:

  Ich wußte, daß es Ihnen gelingen würde.
  I knew you would succeed.

  (iv) After da + preposition:

  Ich verlasse mich darauf, daß Sie mich morgen früh anrufen.
  I rely on your telephoning to-morrow morning.

  (v) After ohne, statt and außer:

  Er hat meine Uhr gestohlen, ohne daß ich's merkte.
  He has stolen my watch without my noticing it.

486. Indem: to be distinguished from während. An indem-clause has the same force as the French *en* + Present Participle. Usually the subject, as well as the time, is the same as that of the main verb:

  Die Deutschen eroberten, indem sie bekehrten.
  The Germans conquered *by converting*.

487. Während:

  (i) Temporal:

  Er entfloh, während ich schlief. He escaped while I slept.

  (ii) Of Contrast:

  Von den zwei Brüdern war der ältere lang und mager, während der jüngere kurz und dick war.
  Of the two brothers the elder was long and thin, *while* (*whereas*) the younger was short and fat.

488. Je:

  Je mehr man ihm gibt, desto mehr verlangt er.
  The more you give him, *the* more he asks.

489. Obgleich, etc. These are often separated:

> Ob ich gleich taub bin,.... Though I am deaf,....

490. Ob. In indirect questions:

> Wissen Sie, ob man hier gut essen kann?
> Do you know whether I can get a good meal here?

In repeating a question which has not been heard aright:

> Sind Sie aus Berlin?—Wie beliebt?—Ob Sie aus Berlin
> sind?
> Are you from Berlin?—I beg your pardon.—Are you
> from Berlin?
> Sind Sie aus Berlin?—Ob ich aus Berlin bin?
> Are you from Berlin?—Am I from Berlin?
> (Colloquially.) Sind Sie hungrig?—Und ob!
> Are you hungry?—Am I not!

491. Wie. Sometimes of time = als, während. More commonly as an adverb of manner or degree, (i) interrogative, (ii) relative:

> Ihr fühlet nicht, wie schlecht ein solches Handwerk sei!
> You do not feel how base is such a trade.
> Ich weiß nicht, wie er ausgesehen hat.
> I don't know how he looked.
> Ein Mann wie Sie. A man like you.
> Weiß wie Schnee. White as snow.
> Sie sind verwundet, wie ich sehe.
> You are wounded, as I see.
> Er starb, wie er gelebt hatte. He died as he had lived.
> Er spricht wie ein Amerikaner.
> He speaks like an American.

Contrast:

> Er spricht als Amerikaner.
> He speaks *as* an American.

X. INTERJECTIONS
(die Interjektion)

492. Interjections may be classified as (*a*) mere sounds used to express emotion, and (*b*) words, phrases, or even short sentences used for the same purpose:

(*a*)

Ach!	Oh!	O je!	O dear, O dear!
Ei!	Oho!	Pfui!	Fie!
He! He da!	Hi! Hallo!	Pst!	(*a*) Hush!
Hurra!	Hurrah!		(*b*) Come here.
Na!	Well.	Wehe!	Woe!
O!	Oh!		

(*b*)

Achtung!	Caution.	Glück auf!	Good luck!
Ade!	(Fr. *adieu*) Farewell.	Halt!	Stop.
		Heil!	Hail.
Auf Wiedersehen!	Au revoir.	Pech!	Hard luck!
Bitte!	Please.	Schade!	What a pity!
Danke!	Thanks. No, thank you.	Vorwärts!	Forward.
Donnerwetter!	By Jove!	Weiter!	Go on.
Fort!	Away!	Willkommen!	Welcome.
Gott sei Dank!	Thank Heaven!	Zu Hilfe!	Help!
Gott bewahre!	God forbid!		

493. Some interjections are followed by cases or prepositional phrases:

Fort mit ihm!	Away with him!
Fort mit Ihnen!	Be off with you!
Heil dem König!	Hail to the King!

XI. ORDER OF WORDS

(die Wortfolge)

I. POSITION OF THE FINITE VERB.

In Main Sentences.

494. In a sentence expressing statement the finite verb comes *second*.

Normally the subject precedes the verb; when any other word comes first, the order of subject and verb is *inverted*.

Almost any part of the sentence may begin it:

The Subject:
Meine Arbeit ist schrecklich.   My work is terrible.

An Object:
Die Jungfrau sah ich nicht.   I did not see the maiden.

A Predicative Noun or Adj.:
Immer ärger ward dieses Wüten gegen die Deutschen.
Worse and worse grew this agitation against the Germans.

An Adverb or Adverb-phrase:
Noch blieb alles still.   Still all was silent.
Nur von Zeit zu Zeit schritt ein Mann durch den Raum.
Only from time to time a man walked across the room.

An Infinitive or Participle:
Arbeiten will er nicht.   Work he will not.

A Subordinate Clause:
Ob ich ein nachdenkliches Gesicht mache, weiß ich nicht.
I do not know if I am looking solemn.
Wenn es regnet, so bleiben wir zu Hause.
If it rains, we shall stay at home.

N.B. After a Concessive Clause, inversion does not always take place:

Wer Sie auch sein mögen, ich lasse Sie nicht herein.
Whoever you may be, I will not let you in.

495. A verb of saying, etc., placed after the quotation, or within it, must precede its subject:

„Wer ist der Herr der Karawane?" fragte der Reiter.
"Who is the master of the caravan?" asked the horseman.

„Da fanden sie," fuhr der Abt fort, „den verstümmelten Leichnam."
"There," the abbot continued, "they found the mutilated corpse."

496. The co-ordinating conjunctions, being merely links and not part of the sentence they introduce, do not entail inversion:

Er ist versetzt worden, und ich bin sitzen geblieben.
He has been promoted and I have been left behind.

497. In sentences expressing Question, Wish, Command, Exclamation, the verb comes before the subject:

Kennst du den Faust?	Knowest thou Faust?
O wäre ich nie geboren!	Would I had never been born!
Kommen Sie bald wieder!	Come back soon.
Wie ist das Leben schön! Wie schön ist das Leben!	How fine life is!

But (i) the normal order is usual with the 3rd person of the Pres. Subj.:

Er lebe hoch!	Long may he live.
Gott sei uns gnädig!	God help us!

(ii) In exclamations the verb is often placed last; see § 498.

In Subordinate Clauses.

498. The verb comes last:

> Ich ging zu Bett, sobald ich mit meiner Arbeit fertig war
> I went to bed as soon as I had finished my work.

Note. Owing to ellipsis of the governing clause, the verb comes last

(i) In Questions repeated (see § 490):

> Essen Sie gern Sauerkraut?—Ob ich gern Sauerkraut esse?
> Do you like Sauerkraut?—Do I like Sauerkraut, did you
>   say?
> (i.e. Fragen Sie, ob ich gern S. esse?)

(ii) Sometimes in Exclamations:

> Wie einsam er gewesen sein mußte!
> How lonely he must have been!
> (i.e. Denken Sie sich nur, wie einsam, usw.)
> Wie schnell der Hund läuft!
> (i.e. Sehen Sie doch, wie schnell, usw.)

499. Some Subordinate Clauses may be expressed by using the inverted order:

(i) *Conditional:*

> Wär' ich besonnen, hieß' ich nicht der Tell.
> *Were* I prudent, my name would not be Tell.

(ii) *Concessive:*

> Ist es gleich Nacht, so leuchtet unser Recht.
> Though it is night, our right shines clear.

500. In Indirect Statement, where daß is not used, the verb is placed as in a main sentence:

> Er sagte, er sei der Herr des Hauses.
> He said he was the master of the house.

II. Position of Infinitives and Participles.

501. In Main Sentences.

Infinitives and participles come last, and in order of importance:

> Wir wollen ein Haus bauen!   Let us build a house.
> Wir werden es bald gebaut haben.
> Es ist noch nicht gebaut worden.
> Wir werden es bauen lassen.
> Es wird gebaut worden sein.

In each case, the inf. or part. of bauen precedes that of the auxiliary; and where there are two auxiliaries, that which immediately governs the effective verb comes next to it.

502. In Subordinate Clauses.

The auxiliary, being the finite verb, comes last:

> Wenn das Haus gebaut worden wäre.
> If the house had been built.

503. In compound tenses of the modal auxiliaries and of lassen, hören, sehen, etc., the auxiliary of tense is displaced and precedes the infinitive:

> Zeige mir, wie ich's hätte bauen sollen.
> Show me how I ought to have built it.

504. Short infinitive phrases may be incorporated in the main sentence; longer ones are usually treated as subordinate clauses:

> Das Mädchen fing zu weinen an.   The girl began to cry.
> Das Mädchen fing an, sich die Augen aus dem Kopfe zu weinen.
> The girl began to cry her eyes out.

III. Position of Adverbs and Adverb Phrases.

505. The general principle is that the most emphatic comes last.   Hence the position of the separable prefixes, and of phrases very closely connected with the verb, such as zu Hilfe, zu Teil, zu Mute.

506. Expressions of Time usually come first; in all other cases the question of emphasis has to be considered:

Er hat mich gestern sehr freundlich gegrüßt.
He greeted me very pleasantly yesterday.

Ich begegnete ihnen gestern auf der Straße.
I met them in the street yesterday.

Wir fahren mit diesem Zuge bis Berlin.
We go as far as Berlin in this train.

Wir haben uns in Wien sehr gut amüsiert.
We had a very good time in Vienna.

In the last example, it would clearly be wrong to separate gut from the verb, with which it goes so closely that we can translate sich gut amüsieren 'to enjoy oneself.'

507. Note that, except in subordinate clauses, the adverb is not placed between subject and verb:

I often see him.   Ich sehe ihn oft.
He then started.   Er machte sich dann auf den Weg.

508. Position of Nicht.

Nicht applying to a word or phrase stands immediately before:

Nicht ganz ist diese Prophezeiung gerechtfertigt worden.
This prophecy was *not entirely* justified.

Nicht die kalten Fürstenherzen sind es, die am meisten verletzen.
It is *not the cold-hearted* princes that inflict most pain.

Er hat nicht meinen Vater gegrüßt.
It was *not my father* that he saluted.

509. Nicht, applying to a whole sentence, comes as late as possible:

Es schneit nicht.   It is not snowing.
Es schneit heute nicht.   It is not snowing to-day.
Es wird heute nicht schneien.   It will not snow to-day.
Er steht heute nicht auf.   He is not getting up to-day.

Er ift heute nicht aufgeftanben.   He has not got up to-day.

Wir haben uns nicht gut amüfiert.

We have not enjoyed ourselves.

Sie werden uns nicht zu Hilfe kommen.

They will not come to our aid.

Er hat meinen Bater nicht gegrüßt.

He has not saluted my father.

Er heißt nicht Müller.   His name is not Müller.

Wir find heute nicht fleißig.   We are not industrious to-day.

510. From these examples it will be seen that nicht comes immediately before the words that usually claim the last place in the clause: Infinitives, Participles; Separable Prefixes and words closely connected with the verb; Predicative Nouns and Adjectives; all of which may be summed up in the word Complement.

We may therefore say that the Complement comes last, and nicht immediately before it.

In subordinate and inverted clauses, the order is exactly the same, except for the position of the finite verb.

In questions, when the verb is in a compound tense, nicht *may* come next to the subject:

Haben Sie nicht ben König gefehen?

Have you not seen the King?

IV. Position of Nouns, Adjectives and Pronouns.

511. A Predicative Noun or Adjective comes as near the end as possible:

Jch bin mit meiner Aufgabe noch nicht fertig.

I have not yet finished my work.

Er war von all meinen Bebienten ber treuefte.

He was the most faithful of all my servants.

512. An Adjective preceding its noun is itself preceded by its modifiers:

Ein in englischen Diensten stehender Italiener.

An Italian in English service.

513. But the modifiers of an adjective or participle separated from its noun may either precede or follow it:

Fest gemauert in der Erden,

Steht die Form, aus Lehm gebrannt.

Firmly bedded in the earth, stands the mould baked of clay.

...unübertroffen in seinen Dispositionen, unerschöpflich in seinen Hilfsmitteln, unerreicht als Führer und Schlachtenherr seiner Truppen.

...unsurpassed in his dispositions, inexhaustible in resources, unequalled as a leader of his troops and commander on the battlefield.

514. A Noun-Object comes after a Pronoun-Object or a short adverb:

Er hat mir einen guten Rat gegeben.

He gave me a piece of good advice.

Wir haben heute kein Frühstück bekommen.

We got no breakfast to-day.

515. In a subordinate clause and in a main clause, where inversion takes place, a Pronoun-Object comes before a Noun-Subject:

Er fragte mich, ob mir der Kaffee geschmeckt habe.

He asked me if I had enjoyed the coffee.

Den nahm mir Gott. God took him from me.

516. Of two Noun-Objects,

(*a*) the person generally comes before the thing;

(*b*) the dative before the accusative;

(*c*) the less emphatic before the more emphatic.

There is therefore considerable latitude in the cases, and no hard-and-fast rule can be stated, e.g.

Was haben Sie Ihren Kindern geschenkt?—Ich habe Wilhelm ein Fahrrad, Emilie ein Halsband und Hans ein Hündchen gegeben.

What did you give your children?—I gave W. a bicycle, E. a necklace, and H. a dog.

Was haben Sie mit Ihrem Geld gemacht?—Ich habe die eine Hälfte einem Bettler gegeben, die andre Hälfte habe ich noch.

What have you done with your money?—I have given half to a beggar; the other half I still have.

517. Of two Pronoun-Objects the less emphatic comes first. Es and the reflexive come before any other Pronouns. The Accusative usually precedes the Dative:

Ich kann es mir nicht leisten.   I cannot afford it.
Ich werde ihn Ihnen vorstellen.   I will introduce him to you.
Ich habe sie ihm geschenkt.   I have given them to him.

But es may come either before or after the reflexive; e.g.
Ich kann mir es nicht leisten.

518. Prepositional phrases usually follow the object:

Ich schreibe eben einen Brief an meinen Vetter.
I am just writing a letter to my cousin.
Der Offizier mußte die Soldaten an ihre Pflicht erinnern.
The officer had to remind the soldiers of their duty.

XII. WORD FORMATION

(die Wortbildung)

519. Derivatives are formed in four ways:

    (i) by simple vowel-change, Umlaut or Ablaut,
    (ii) by prefix,
    (iii) by suffix,
    (iv) by joining two words together.

520. (i) VOWEL-CHANGE.

    (*a*) **Ablaut.** Nouns from Verb-stems:

brechen, der Bruch, fracture	sprechen, der Spruch, saying
fliegen, der Flug, flight	singen, der Sang, song
binden, der Bund, bond	binden, das Band, fetter
springen, der Sprung, spring	beißen, der Biß, bite.

In many cases the verb-stem remains unaltered:

der Schlag, blow	der Lauf, course
der Rat, advice	der Ruf, call.

521. (*b*) **Umlaut.** Factitive verbs:

fahren, drive, führen, lead; wachen, watch, wecken, wake; fallen, fall, fällen, fell; hangen, hang (intrans.), hängen, hang (trans.); liegen, lie, legen, lay; sinken, sink (intrans.), senken, sink (trans.); sitzen, sit, setzen, set; springen, spring, sprengen, explode, sprinkle.

    (ii) PREFIXES.

522. Prefixes are either stressed or unstressed.

The Unstressed Prefixes are be=, emp=, ent=, er=, ge=, miß=, ver=, zer=.

523. **Be-** (*a*) makes intransitive verbs transitive:

    weinen, weep; beweinen, to weep for.
    gehen, go; ein Verbrechen begehen, to commit a crime.

(*b*) alters the direction of transitive verbs:

ein Lieb fingen, to sing a song; einen Helben befingen, to sing of a hero; ein Buch fchreiben, to write a book; eine Lanbfchaft befchreiben, to write about (i.e. describe) a landscape; fchießen, to shoot, befchießen, to bombard.

(*c*) forms verbs from nouns:

bewaffnen, to arm	beeinfluffen, to influence
belaften, to burden	befohlen, to sole (a shoe).

Note the participial forms:

begabt, talented	begütert, possessing property
bemittelt, possessing means	benachbart, neighbouring
berebt, eloquent	bewölft, cloudy
bewußt, conscious.	

524. Emp-, ent- (emp- occurs only in empfangen, empfehlen, empfinben):

(*a*) origin:

entftehen, originate	entfprießen, entfpringen, spring
entbrennen, catch fire	entflammen, entzünben, kindle.

(*b*) removal, separation, deprivation:

entgehen, entlaufen, entfommen, escape; entwickeln, develop; enterben, disinherit; entlarven, unmask; fich enthalten, abstain; entwaffnen, disarm; entfalten, unfold; entfetzen, depose; entfchulbigen, excuse.

525. Er-: (*a*) achievement:

ereilen	overtake	erfechten	win by fighting
erringen	win by effort	erwerben	win by industry
erfchlagen	kill	erfchießen	shoot dead
erftechen	stab to death	ermorben	murder.

(*b*) the completion of a process; and so the beginning of a new state:

erſterben	die out	ertrinken	drown
erlöſchen	be extinguished	erfolgen	succeed
erröten	blush	erneuern	renew
erſchrecken	to be startled	erwachſen	to grow up.

526. Ge-: (*a*) original meaning *together*:

der Gefährte	companion	der Geſpiele	playmate
der Genoſſe	companion	der Gevatter	godfather (cf. *compère*)
der Geſelle	companion (from Saal)	das Gewiſſen,	Lat. *conscientia*.

(*b*) forms collective nouns:

das Gebirge	mountain-range	das Geſpann	team of horses, etc.
das Geſträuch	undergrowth	das Getreide	corn
das Geſtrüpp	undergrowth	das Gehirn	brain.

(*c*) verbal nouns:

das Gebet	prayer	das Gefecht	battle
der Geruch	smell	der Geſang	song
das Gehör	sense of hearing	das Geſchrei	shout.

527. Miß-, *wrongly, amiss*:

mißbrauchen, abuse   mißverſtehen, misunderstand.

528. Ver-: (*a*) *Away*, either literally, of place, or metaphorically, *out of existence*:

verreiſen	to travel away	verſenden	send away
verpfänden	give as pledge	vergehen	pass away
verſprechen	promise	verſchwinden	vanish
verderben	destroy	verſpielen	lose (one's money)
verhallen }	die away (of		at play
verſchallen }	sound)	verlernen	unlearn, forget.

(*b*) deterioration:

verkommen, to go to the dogs	verrufen, to speak ill of, defame
verpfuschen, spoil by bungling	verraten, betray
verkehren, turn around (past part. verkehrt, wrong).	

Especially with reflexive verbs:

sich verspielen, play a wrong note
sich versingen, sing a wrong note
sich verlaufen, lose one's way
sich verrechnen, make a miscalculation
sich den Fuß vertreten, sprain one's ankle.
Ich habe mich versprochen.   It was a slip of the tongue.

529. **Zer-**, *asunder, to pieces*:

zergliedern	analyse	zerreißen	tear to pieces
zerlumpt	tattered	zerschlagen	smash
zerstreuen	scatter	zertreten	crush
zerstreut	absent-minded	zerquetschen	squash.

530. In the case of the **Stressed Prefixes**, the meaning is usually fairly clear; but they are the province of the dictionary rather than the grammar. A short list appears in § 269.

There remain however two which are not prefixed to verbs, u n≠ and u r≠.

531. **An-**, generally stressed before nouns, adjectives, and adverbs; unstressed before participles and adjectives derived from verbs:

(*a*) English *un-*:

die Únschuld	innocence	unerhórt	unheard of
der Únsinn	nonsense	unéndlich	infinite
únnütz	useless	úngewiß	uncertain
unbénkbar	unthinkable	unmóglich	impossible.

(*b*) before Nouns, *enormous*:

eine Unmenge, a vast quantity   eine Unmaſſe, a huge mass

eine Untiefe, an enormous depth   eine Unſumme, a huge sum.

(*c*) before Nouns, *evil*:

das Unkraut, weed   der Unmenſch, inhuman monster

der Unfug, disorder   das Ungeziefer, vermin.

532. Ur-, *original, very old*:

uralt, as old as the hills   der Urwald, primeval forest

das Urbild, prototype   der Urheber, the instigator

der Ursprung, origin   die Ursache, cause.

(iii) (*a*) SUFFIXES USED FOR FORMING NOUNS.

533. -chen, -lein, added to nouns, form diminutives (all neuter):

das Männchen, Männlein, man   das Häuschen, Häuslein, house

das Vöglein, bird   das Mädchen, Mägdlein, girl.

The idea of smallness is not always implied; diminutives are often terms of endearment, or of contempt. They are much used in family life:

Väterchen, Mütterchen, Kindchen, Tantchen, uſw.

534. -e added to verb-stems or roots:

die Gabe, gift   die Frage, question

die Lage, situation   die Strafe, punishment;

to adjectives (with Umlaut):

die Länge, length   die Breite, breadth   die Kälte, cold

die Fläche, surface   die Höhe, height   die Wärme, heat.

535. -ei (*a*) added to masc. nouns to denote occupation, thence to scene of occupation:

die Abtei, abbacy, abbey   die Bäckerei, bakery

die Malerei, painting   die Einſiedelei, hermitage;

or collectively, die Reiterei cavalry.

(*b*) often with a depreciatory meaning, especially when it appears as the double suffix ⸗erei :

die Spielerei, nonsense	die Kinderei, childishness
die Büberei, roguery	die Klimperei, strumming
die Quacksalberei quackery.	(on piano).

Compare the English *foolery, finery, trumpery*, etc.

536. -el added usually to verb-roots, to denote a means :

der Flügel (fliegen), wing	der Schlüssel (schließen), key
der Hebel (heben), lever	der Deckel (decken), lid
der Klingel (klingen), bell	der Zügel (ziehen), rein.

537. -er, -ler, -ner :

(*a*) added to verbs to denote an agent or instrument :

der Bäcker, baker	der Führer, leader
der Schneider, tailor	der Schläger, rapier
der Maler, painter	der Vergaser, carburetter.

(*b*) added to nouns to denote origin or other connection :

der Engländer, Englishman	der Gärtner, gardener
	der Schüler, scholar.

(*c*) ⸗ler and ⸗ner are variants of ⸗er :

der Lügner, liar	der Redner, orator
der Söldner, mercenary soldier	der Vierfüßler, quadruped
der Ausflügler, excursionist	der Autler, motorist
der Sommerfrischler, summer holiday-maker.	

538. -heit, -keit, added to adjectives, form abstract nouns :

(*a*) ⸗keit is used with adjectives in ⸗el, ⸗er, ⸗bar, ⸗ig, ⸗lich, ⸗sam ; also, with inserted ⸗ig, with those in ⸗haft, ⸗los :

die Eitelkeit, vanity	die Heiterkeit, cheerfulness
die Heftigkeit, violence	die Sparsamkeit, economy
die Schamhaftigkeit, modesty	die Furchtlosigkeit, fearlessness.

(*b*) ⸗heit added to other adjectives or nouns :

die Weisheit, wisdom   die Torheit, folly.

539. **-in** added to names of male beings, usually with Umlaut:

die Königin, queen   die Amerikanerin, American woman
die Tänzerin, dancer   die Löwin, lioness.

Nouns in -e drop the -e and add -in without Umlaut:

der Sklave, die Sklavin, slave; der Russe, die Russin, Russian.

But der Franzose, Frenchman, gives die Französin.

540. **-ing, -ling** added to various parts of speech:

der Dichterling, poetaster   der Frühling, spring
der Jüngling, youth   der Zwilling, twin
der Findling, foundling   der Höfling, courtier
der Schwächling, weakling.

541. **-nis** added to adjectives and verbs:

das Gefängnis, prison   das Gedächtnis, memory
die Kenntnis, information   die Wildnis, wilderness.

542. **-sal, -sel** added to verbs:

das Rätsel, riddle   das Schicksal, fate
das Scheusal, horror   das Drangsal, oppression.

543. **-schaft** added to nouns, occasionally to adjectives and participles:

die Freundschaft, friendship   die Knechtschaft, serfdom
die Mannschaft, crew   die Bürgschaft, surety
die Gefangenschaft, captivity.

544. **-st, -t**, added to verb-stems, form fem. nouns:

die Schrift, writing; die Kunst, art; die Ankunft, arrival; but der Dienst, service.

545. **-tum** added to nouns and adjectives, to form abstract and a few collective nouns. All but two are neuter:

der Irrtum, the error   der Reichtum, wealth
das Deutschtum, German character   das Priestertum, priestly office

bas Königtum, royalty   bas Altertum, antiquity
bas Heiligtum, sanctuary   bas Eigentum, property
bas Christentum, Christianity bas Bürgertum, citizenship.

Note: bie Christenheit, Christendom; bie Priesterschaft, the
clergy (collectively); bie Eigenschaft, quality; bas Königreich,
kingdom.

546. **-ung** forms verbal nouns:

bie Krönung, coronation   bie Heizung, heating
bie Nahrung, nourishment   bie Erfindung, invention
bie Beobachtung, observation   bie Beschreibung, description.

Note that many of these nouns have acquired a concrete
meaning, e.g. bie Erfindung may stand for the *thing* invented;
bie Nahrung for the actual *food* consumed.

(*b*) SUFFIXES USED FOR FORMING ADJECTIVES.

547. **-bar** added to verbs, sometimes to nouns and adjectives:

eßbar, edible   benkbar, conceivable   haltbar, tenable
brauchbar, bienstbar, serviceable   waschbar, washable
fruchtbar, fertile   furchtbar, terrible offenbar, evident.

548. **-en, -ern**, *made of*:

golben, golden   hölzern, wooden   eifern, iron
lebern, of leather wollen, woollen   papiern, paper.

549. **-haft** mainly with nouns, also with adjectives and verbs:

mannhaft, manly   sünbhaft, sinful   krankhaft, morbid
scherzhaft, jesting schamhaft, modest schmeichelhaft, flattering.
tugenbhaft, virtuous.

550. **-ig** with nouns, adjectives or adverbs:

blutig, bloody   lustig, merry   mächtig, mighty
gütig, kind   freubig, joyful   sonnig, sunny
mutig, courageous völlig, complete   jetzig, present
hiesig, of this place bortig, of that place bamalig, of that time.
      (Der bamalige Bürgermeister. The then mayor.)

551. **-iſch**, with proper names:

römiſch, Roman   franzöſiſch, French   fränkiſch, Frankish
indiſch, Indian   europäiſch, European   Müllerſch, of or pertaining to Müller.

With other nouns, usually (but not always) depreciatory:

kindiſch childish   neidiſch envious   maleriſch picturesque
tieriſch bestial   mürriſch surly   künſtleriſch artistic.

552. **-lich** = *-like*, *-ly*, added to nouns, adjectives, or verb-stems:

väterlich, paternal, fatherly   weiblich, feminine, womanly
kaiſerlich, imperial   freundlich, friendly
jährlich, annual, yearly   wöchentlich, weekly
rötlich, reddish   ältlich, oldish, elderly
erträglich, tolerable   beträchtlich, considerable
ſterblich, mortal   unſäglich, unutterable.

553. **-los** = Eng. *-less*, added to nouns:

ſchuldlos, guiltless   hirnlos, brainless
arbeitslos, unemployed   heimatlos, homeless.

554. **-mäßig**, *in accordance with*:

regelmäßig, regular   vorſchriftsmäßig, regulation.

555. **-ſam** = Eng. *-some*, added to nouns, adjectives and verbs:

furchtſam, timid   biegſam, pliant
folgſam, docile   gehorſam, obedient
ſchweigſam, silent   regſam, lively
langſam, slow   einſam, lonely.

(c) THE SUFFIX -ier(en).

556. This is added to foreign verb-stems, sometimes even to German words (hantieren, handle; buchſtabieren, spell):

ſpazieren, take a walk   exerzieren, drill
ſtudieren, study   ſich genieren, to be shy (*se géner*)
analyſieren, analyse   oxydieren, oxidise.

English verbs usually naturalise without -ieren:

boxen, box; ſtarten, start; ſtreiken, strike (industrially).

(iv) (*a*) COMPOUND NOUNS.

557. Compounds may be classified:

(*a*) **Two Nouns:**

der Hausherr, master of the house

der Sauhirt, swineherd

der Schauspieler, actor

der Tierarzt, veterinary

der Kuhstall, cow-house

das Kindermädchen, nursemaid

das Volkslied, folk-song.

Feminine nouns standing as the first part of a compound usually add -s or -en:

der Geburtstag, birthday

der Liebesbrief, love-letter

die Arbeitsliebe, love of work

der Sonnenaufgang, sunrise.

558. (*b*) **Adjective + Noun:**

der Junker (Jung=herr), squire

der Schwarzwald, Black Forest

der Rotwein, red wine

der Edelmann, nobleman

das Dreieck, triangle

das Kleingeld, change.

Hoch, neu, alt appear very frequently in such compounds:

Hochachtung, esteem; Hochaltar, high altar; Hochamt, High Mass; Hochgeboren, your lordship; Hochstapler, swell criminal, etc. Any dictionary will give a number of such examples.

559. (*c*) **Verb-stem + Noun:**

das Trinkwasser, drinking-water

die Reitpeitsche, riding-whip

das Lesebuch, reader

das Trinkgeld, tip (cf. *pourboire*).

(*b*) COMPOUND ADJECTIVES.

560. (*a*) **Noun + Adjective,**

(i) the noun being governed by the adjective:

wasserreich, well-watered

wasserdicht, waterproof

lebensfroh cheerful

sorgenfrei, care-free

arbeitslustig, industrious

geisteskrank, insane;

(ii) the noun expressing a comparison:

riefengroß, gigantic	blitzſchnell, quick as lightning
pechfinſter, black as pitch	rabenſchwarz, raven-black
ſchneeweiß, snow-white	ſteinreich, rich as Crœsus
blutarm, poor as a church mouse	blutjung, in the bloom of youth
	ſteinhart, hard as stone

mäuschenſtill, quiet as a mouse.

In (i) the stress accent falls on the first syllable; in (ii) there is almost equal stress on each component of the adjective; thus blútarm ('blu·t'arm) means 'poor *in* blood, anæmic,' whereas blútárm ('blu·t''arm) means 'poor *as* blood,' i.e. 'very poor indeed.' Similarly, ſteínreich ('staⁱnraⁱç) means 'rich in stones'; ſteínreích ('staⁱn'raⁱç) 'as rich as can be'; ſteínhárt ('staⁱn'hart) 'as hard as stone.'

561. (*b*) **Adjective + Adjective:**

hellgrün, light green	dunkelrot, dark red
tollkühn, foolhardy	bitterſüß, bitter-sweet.

562. (*c*) **Adjective + Noun + ⸗ig** (or ⸗iſch):

blauäugig, blue-eyed	einhändig, one-handed
kurzſichtig, short-sighted	langbeinig, long-legged
zweiſilbig, disyllabic	alt⸗ } modiſch {old- } fashioned. neu⸗} {new-}

XIII. SUBORDINATE CLAUSES

563. A Subordinate Clause is Substantival, Adjectival or Adverbial, according as it performs the functions of a Noun, an Adjective or an Adverb.

564. A SUBSTANTIVAL CLAUSE may be

(*a*) Subject:

Daß er heute kommt, ist sicher.
That he will come to-day is certain.
Ob er bis morgen bleiben kann, ist zweifelhaft.
Whether he can stay till to-morrow is doubtful.

Or, with anticipatory es:

Es ist sicher, daß... Es ist zweifelhaft, ob...

565. (*b*) Object:

Ich glaube, daß er mich betrügt.
I think he is deceiving me.
Ich fragte ihn, wohin er gehe.
I asked him where he was going.
Ich wünschte, er könnte bleiben.   I wish he could stay.

See §§ 341–349.

566. (*c*) Governed by a Preposition. In this case, the Noun-Clause is anticipated by da, which is then combined with the Preposition, so that the clause is really in apposition to the da:

Er besteht darauf, daß ich mitgehe.
He insists on my going with him.
Es kommt darauf an, ob es regnet.
It depends whether it rains.
Wer steht mir dafür, daß er reich ist?
Who guarantees that he is rich?

Er ärgert mich dadurch, daß er so schlechte Kleider trägt.
He annoys me by wearing such bad clothes.

But ohne, anstatt are followed directly by a daß=clause:

Er ist entflohen, ohne daß ich es wußte (or wüßte).
He escaped without my knowing it.

See § 377.

567. An ADJECTIVAL CLAUSE contains a Relative Pronoun or Relative Adverb.

568. (a) Glücklich allein ist die Seele, die liebt!
Happy is none but the soul that loves.
Das ist der Mann, den ich suche.
That is the man I seek.
Das wissen wir, die wir die Gemsen jagen.
We who hunt the chamois know that.

See §§ 191, 192.

Note the use of wer and was as Relatives, or Relative + Demonstrative:

Wer nicht hören will, der muß fühlen.
He who will not hear must feel.
Wer sich nicht raten läßt, dem kann man nicht helfen.
He who will not be advised cannot be helped.
Er tut, was er kann.   He does what he can.

See §§ 199, 200.

569. (b) Relative Adverb equivalent to Preposition + Rel. Pronoun:

Kling hinaus bis an das Haus,   Wo die Blumen sprießen.
Let thy strains reach the house where the flowers bloom
(wo = an welchem, or um welches).
In dem Lande, wohin er auswanderte, geht es ihm gut.
In the country to which he emigrated he is prospering.

Note the relative use of wie with or without a Personal Pronoun to complete the clause:

Es ist, wie ich dir sagte.   It is as I told you.

Das sind Kinder, wie ich sie gern sehe.

Those are the sort of children that I like.

Er zeigte eine Rührung, wie jener kleine Dienst sie gar nicht wert war.

He showed such emotion as that small service had not merited.

Er hatte große, weite Pantoffeln an, wie ich sie sonst nie gesehen.

He wore great wide slippers such as I had never seen before.

See § 221.

Mood in Relative Clauses.

570. The Indicative is used, except where there is an implication (*a*) of Purpose, (*b*) of Unreality:

   (*a*) Schickt einen sichern Boten ihm entgegen,

       Der auf geheimem Weg ihn zu mir führe.

       Send a sure messenger to meet him, to guide him to me by a secret path.

This use is rare. The Infinitive should be used where possible, otherwise sollen.

   (*b*) In Goethes Werken ist keine Zeile, deren Wahrheit er nicht selbst erfahren hätte.

       In Goethe's works there is not a line of which he had not himself experienced the truth.

       Wenn er Geld hätte, so würde er alle beschenken, die ihn um Almosen bäten.

       If he had any money, he would give to all who asked him for alms.

But   Er beschenkt alle, die ihn um Almosen bitten.

See § 338.

571. ADVERBIAL CLAUSES may be classified as clauses of Place, Time, Manner, Degree, Comparison, Consequence, Cause, Purpose, Condition, Concession. In many cases however there is no sharp line of demarcation between these classes, e.g.

Er verließ uns, indem er heftige Drohungen ausstieß.
Uttering violent threats, he left us (Time or Manner).

Er läuft, wie ein Reh. He runs like a deer; *either* he runs as a deer runs (Manner), *or* he runs as fast as a deer (Degree).

572. 1. **Place.** Conjunctions wo, woher, wohin:

Ich fand ihn, wo ich ihn suchte.
I found him where I sought him.

573. 2. **Time.** Conjunctions als, wenn, da, indem, während, wie, sobald, solange; bis, ehe, bevor; nachdem, seit, seitdem:

Indem wir sprechen, verrinnt die Zeit.
Even while we speak, the time is fleeting.

Wir warteten, bis er ankam. We waited till he arrived.

For the distinction between wenn and als, see § 481.

The verb is usually in the Indicative. The Subj. is used to express a contingency imagined, and not yet realised:

Wir warteten, bis er ankäme. We waited for him to come.

574. 3. **Manner.** Conjunctions als, wie, indem:

Ich singe, wie der Vogel singt. I sing as the bird sings.
Die Deutschen eroberten, indem sie bekehrten.
The Germans conquered by converting.

Contracted forms are common:

Du bist wie eine Blume (ist). Thou art like a flower.
Ich folge dir, als meinem Führer. I follow you as my leader.

See § 491.

13-3

575. 4. **Degree.** Conjunctions als, wie:

Sie sind sich so ähnlich, wie ein Ei dem andern (ähnlich ist).

They are as like as two peas.

Er hat heute besser gespielt, als (er) gestern (gespielt hat).

He played better to-day than yesterday.

Als is used for comparison of superiority or inferiority; wie for comparison of equality:

Er hat heute nicht so gut gespielt, als gestern.

Er hat heute ebenso gut gespielt, wie gestern.

576. 5. **Comparison, Proportion.** Conjunctions als wenn, als ob, je...je, je...desto, je...um so, je nachdem:

Tun Sie, als wenn Sie zu Hause wären.

Make yourself at home.

Mir ist, als wären wir im Paradies.

I feel as if we were in Paradise.

Je mehr ich dieses Gedicht studiere, desto weniger verstehe ich es.

The more I study this poem, the less I understand it.

Je länger, je lieber. The longer the better.

Du wirst gelobt, je nachdem du es verdienst.

You will be praised according to your merit.

577. 6. **Consequence.** Conjunctions daß, so...daß, sodaß, als daß. Actual Consequence, Indicative; Potential Consequence, Subjunctive:

Sie goß Wasser in die Pfanne, daß eine mächtige Wolke emporstieg.

She poured water into the pan, so that a dense cloud rose from it.

Er wandte sich schnell zur Seite, sodaß ich ihn nicht fassen konnte.

He swerved quickly, so that I could not seize him.

Er ist zu klug, als daß er an Gespenster glauben sollte.

He is too clever to believe in ghosts.

Er hat mich zu tief gekränkt, als daß ich ihm verzeihen könnte.

He has hurt me too deeply for me to forgive him.

Contractions, when the subject is the same for both verbs:

Er ist zu klug, um an Gespenster zu glauben.

Er ist alt genug, um für sich selbst zu sprechen.

Es ist zum Überschnappen.   It is enough to drive one mad.

N.B. Seien Sie so freundlich und setzen Sie sich! (or Haben Sie die Güte, sich zu setzen!) Be so kind as to sit down.

578. 7. Cause. Conjunctions weil, da, nun:

Warum arbeiten Sie nicht?—Weil ich krank bin.

Why are you not working?—Because I am ill.

Ich kann nicht arbeiten, da ich krank bin.

I cannot work, as I am ill.

Was kann dich ängstigen, nun du mich kennst?

What can trouble you, now that you know me?

579. 8. Purpose. Conjunctions daß, damit.

The verb is in the Subj. But instead of the *Pres.* Subj. it is permissible to use either the Pres. Ind. or können with Inf.:

Er arbeitete, damit seine Kinder zu essen hätten.

He worked in order that his children might have food.

Euch künd' ich's an, damit ihr's alle wisset.

To you I proclaim it, that you may all know.

Kommen Sie näher, damit ich Sie sehen kann.

Come closer, so that I may see you.

Geh ihm aus dem Weg, damit er dir nichts zuleide tut.

Get out of his way, lest he do you an injury.

The contracted form with um...zu is allowed when both verbs have the same subject:

Was habt ihr denn getan, um sie zu retten?

What have you done to save her?

Man muß säen, um zu ernten.

One must sow in order to reap.

When the idea of purpose is obvious, um is often omitted:

Ich komme nicht, zu bleiben; Abschied zu nehmen, komm' ich.

I come not to stay; to take my leave I come.

See §§ 361, 363.

580. 9. **Condition.** Conjunctions wenn, falls:

Wenn es regnet, (so) werden wir zu Hause bleiben.

If it rains, we shall stay at home.

Wenn ich Zeit hätte, so würde ich ihn besuchen.

If I had time, I should call on him.

Wenn ich Zeit gehabt hätte, so { würde ich ihn besucht haben.
{ hätte ich ihn besucht.

If I had had time, I should have called on him.

Ich werde dir helfen, falls es nötig sein sollte.

I will help you, in case it should be necessary.

Condition may be expressed by inversion:

Hätte ich Zeit,... Hätte ich Zeit gehabt,... Sollte es regnen,...

See §§ 334, 352, 353.

581. 10. **Concession.** Concessive clauses are mainly of two
         types:

   (a) Conditional, introduced by und wenn, or by wenn or ob,
       followed by auch, gleich, schon, or wohl (see § 480):

Wir folgen dir, und wenn's zur Hölle ginge.

We'll follow you, though it should be to Hell.

Sie sind mir bekannt, obwohl Sie mich nicht kennen.

You are known to me, though you do not know me.

Contracted:

Obwohl schon mißmutig geworden, entschloß er sich doch, diesen
letzten Versuch zu machen.

Though he had now lost heart, he nevertheless resolved to
make this last attempt.

Inverted Order instead of wenn, etc.:

Iſt es gleich Nacht, ſo leuchtet unſer Recht.

Though it is night, our right shines clear as day.

582. (*b*) Interrogative, marked by wer, was, wie, wo, etc.:

Was es auch ſei, dein Leben ſichr' ich dir.

Whatever it may be, I promise you your life.

Wo er auch ſei (or ſein mag), ich werde ihn zu finden wiſſen.

Wherever he may be, I shall contrive to find him.

Was er auch ſchweres mag verſchuldet haben, Strafe genug iſt
ſein entſeßlich Handwerk.

Whatever grievous crime he may have committed, his
dreadful trade is punishment enough.

Before an adjective or adverb, ſo is often used instead of wie:

Vater und Mutter werden mich ziehen laſſen, ſo ſchwer es ihnen
wird.

Father and Mother will let me go, hard as it will be for
them.

Ich muß heute ſchon abreiſen, ſo ſehr { ich es auch bedauere.
{ es mir leid tut.

I must leave to-day, much as it grieves me.

See also § 332.

APPENDIX

DECLENSION OF NOUNS.

Alternative to §§ 44—59.

44. There are two Declensions, the Strong and the Weak.
Weak Nouns admit of one termination only, ⸗en, or ⸗n.
Strong Nouns add ⸗es or ⸗s in the Genitive Singular. The
Nominative Plural is usually formed by adding ⸗e.

45. In *all* Nouns the Accusative and Genitive Plural are the
same as the Nominative Plural, and the Dative Plural
ends in ⸗n. Where the Nom. Pl. ends in ⸗n, the Dative
has no further termination, e.g.

> N., A., G. die Pulte; D. den Pulten.
> N., A., G. die Fräulein; D. den Fräulein.

46. *All* Feminine Nouns are invariable in the Singular, and
are therefore excepted from any general rules as to terminations in the Singular.

47. Umlaut in Nouns.

In very many Strong Nouns the root-vowel is modified in
the plural, a, au, o, u becoming ä, äu, ö, ü respectively. No
universal rule can be laid down, but it is useful to remember
that, *without exception*, modification takes place in

> All plurals in -er; All fem. plurals in -e;
> No plurals in -n; No neut. plurals in -e.

48. Compound Nouns are declined as the last component:

der Eingang, entrance, die Eingänge; das Weinglas, wine-
glass, die Weingläser.

Compounds of Mann, however, usually take Leute in the Plural:

der Hauptmann, captain, die Hauptleute; der Seemann, sea-
man, die Seeleute; der Kaufmann, merchant, die Kaufleute.

Note Staatsmänner, statesmen; Ehemänner, husbands; Ehe⸗
leute, married people.

49. WEAK DECLENSION.

Sing. N.	der Haſe	der Held	die		die	
A.	den Haſen	den Helden	die	⎱Roſe	die	⎱Herrin
G.	des Haſen	des Helden	der		der	
D.	dem Haſen	dem Helden	der		der	
Plur. N.	die	die	die		die	
A.	die ⎱Haſen	die ⎱Helden	die ⎱Roſen		die ⎱Herrinnen.	
G.	der	der	der		der	
D.	den	den	den		den	

Note (i) the doubling of the n in the plurals of feminines
in ‑in; (ii) that feminines in ‑e, ‑el, ‑er add ‑n, and not ‑en, in
the plural.

50. *To this declension belong*

(*a*) All Masculines in ‑e, except der Käſe, cheese, and nine
others, which are strong; see § 57.

(*b*) The following Masculines, which have lost the final ‑e:

Ochs, Hirt, Menſch,	Ox, herdsman, man,
Graf, Held, Herr,	count, hero, lord,
Fürſt, Prinz, Geck,	prince, prince, fop,
Spatz, Fink, Bär,	sparrow, finch, bear,
Vorfahr, Ahn,	forefather, ancestor,
Geſell, Chriſt, Mohr,	fellow, Christian, Moor,
Hageſtolz, Schenk,	bachelor, butler,
Lump, Narr, Tor.	rascal, fool, fool.

(*c*) The following Feminines:

Art, Form, Zahl,	Kind, form, number,
Welt, Zeit, Uhr,	world, time, clock,
Schuld, Laſt, Qual,	debt, burden, torment,
Poſt, Bahn, Spur,	post, way, track,
Pflicht, Tat, Wahl,	duty, deed, choice,
Jagd, Saat, Flur,	hunt, young corn, field,
Frau, Schar, Schlacht,	woman, host, battle,
Burg, Tür, Tracht,	castle, door, costume,
Schrift, Fahrt, Flut,	writing, journey, flood,
Bucht, Brut, Schlucht, Glut.	bight, brood, ravine, glow.

(*d*) All Feminines of more than one syllable, except

    (i)   those in ⸗nis and ⸗fal, see § 55 ;

    (ii) Mutter and Tochter, see § 56.

51. STRONG DECLENSION.

  I. NOUNS OF ONE SYLLABLE.

Sing.	N.	der Zug	die ⎫		das Pult
	A.	den Zug	die ⎪	Hand	das Pult
	G.	des Zuges	der ⎪		des Pultes
	D.	dem Zuge	der ⎭		dem Pulte
Plur.	N.	die Züge	die Hände		die Pulte
	A.	die Züge	die Hände		die Pulte
	G.	der Züge	der Hände		der Pulte
	D.	den Zügen	den Händen		den Pulten.

Note. The ⸗e of the Gen. and Dat. Sing. is optional; but after a sibilant (s, ß, sch, z) or st, the Gen. must end in ⸗es and the Dat. in ⸗e.

Umlaut takes place in most masculines, all feminines, no neuters.

52. EXCEPTIONS.

  A. The following masculines do not modify:

Akt, Takt, Laut, Hall,	Act, bar (music), sound, sound,
Stoff, Druck, Schuft, Knall,	stuff, pressure, rogue, report,
Huf, Schuh, Arm, Hund,	hoof, shoe, arm, dog,
Dachs, Lachs, Hauch, Mund,	badger, salmon, breath, mouth,
Mond, Tag, Aar,	moon, day, eagle,
Horst, Punkt, Grab,	eyrie, point, degree,
Dolch, Dom, Star,	dagger, cathedral, starling,
Halm, Gau, Pfad.	stalk, district, path.

Also the following, which do not occur without prefixes:

Besuch, Gesuch, Versuch,	Visit, request, attempt,
Erfolg, Gemahl, Verlust.	success, husband, loss.

53. *B.* The following form the Plural by modifying and adding ⸗er :

Masculines:

Geiſt, Gott, Leib, Mann,	Spirit, God, body, man,
Wald, Wurm, Rand.	wood, worm, edge.

Neuters:

Ei, Neſt, Huhn,	Egg, nest, fowl,
Volk, Weib, Kind,	folk, woman, child,
Haupt, Maul, Horn,	head, mouth, horn,
Lamm, Kalb, Rind,	lamb, calf, ox,
Dorf, Gut, Land, Feld,	village, farm, land, field,
Schloß, Haus, Pfand, Geld,	mansion, house, pledge, money,
Korn, Blatt, Kraut, Gras,	corn, leaf, herb, grass,
Reis, Tal, Grab, Glas,	twig, valley, grave, glass,
Tuch, Kleid, Loch, Dach,	cloth, garment, hole, roof,
Holz, Brett, Faß, Fach,	wood, board, cask, shelf,
Licht, Amt, Schwert, Glied, Rad,	light, office, sword, limb, wheel,
Bild, Buch, Wort, Lied, Bad.	picture, book, word, song, bath.

Also with prefix Ge⸗ :

Gehalt, Gemach, Gemüt,	Salary, room, temperament,
Geſchlecht, Geſicht, Geſpenſt,	race, face, ghost,
Gewand.	robe.

54. *C.* Der Fels is declined as from a Nom. Sing. Felſen, Gen. Felſens; all other cases Felſen.

Das Herz has Acc. Sing. Herz, Gen. Sing. Herzens; all other cases Herzen.

II. Nouns of two or more Syllables.

55. *A.* Those in ⸗ig, ⸗ich, ⸗ing, ⸗nis, ⸗ſal, form their plurals in ⸗e without Umlaut:

		crane	wilderness		fate
Sing.	N.	der Kranich	die ⎫		das Schickſal
	A.	den Kranich	die ⎬ Wildnis		das Schickſal
	G.	des Kranichs	der ⎪		des Schickſals
	D.	dem Kranich	der ⎭		dem Schickſal

Plur.   N.   die Kraniche   die Wildnisse   die Schicksale
       A.   die Kraniche   die Wildnisse   die Schicksale
       G.   der Kraniche   der Wildnisse   der Schicksale
       D.   den Kranichen   den Wildnissen   den Schicksalen.

Note that nouns in ⸗nis double the s before a termination: das Zeugnis, testimony; des Zeugnisses, die Zeugnisse.

Similarly the masculines:

Abend, Amboß, Kompaß,	Evening, anvil, compass,
Leichnam, Eidam, Monat,	corpse, son-in-law, month,
Heißsporn, Unhold, Vielfraß.	hotspur, monster, glutton.

56.   *B.* Masculines and Neuters in ⸗el, ⸗en, ⸗er, and Neuter Diminutives in ⸗chen and ⸗lein drop the ⸗e of the termination wherever it occurs. They have therefore no termination except the ⸗s of the Gen. Sing. and the ⸗n of the Dat. Plural. Those ending in ⸗n take no termination in the Dat. Plural. The majority do not modify:

Sing.   der Sommer   das Wunder   das Fräulein
        den Sommer   das Wunder   das Fräulein
        des Sommers   des Wunders   des Fräuleins
        dem Sommer   dem Wunder   dem Fräulein

Plur.   die Sommer   die Wunder   die ⎫
       die Sommer   die Wunder   die ⎬ Fräulein.
       der Sommer   der Wunder   der ⎪
       den Sommern   den Wundern   den ⎭

The following modify in the plural:

The Masculines:

Ofen, Sattel, Mantel,	Oven, saddle, cloak,
Vogel, Schnabel, Handel,	bird, beak, business,
Nagel, Hammer, Mangel, Faden,	nail, hammer, want, thread,
Garten, Boden, Apfel, Laden,	garden, ground, apple, shop,

Acker, Hafen, Graben, Schaden,   field, haven, ditch, harm,
Vater, Bruder, Schwager,   father, brother, brother-in-law,
and the Neuter Kloſter, monastery.

Pl. Öfen, Sättel, Mäntel, etc.

Similarly the two Feminines Mutter, mother, and Tochter, daughter. Pl. Mütter, Töchter.

57. *C.* Seven Masculines in ⸗e form their other cases as from a Nom. in ⸗en:

Friede, Funke, Glaube, Name,   Peace, spark, faith, name,
Haufe, Wille, Same.   heap, will, seed.

Gen. Sing. Friedens, Funkens, etc. All other cases Frieden, Funken, etc.

Similarly the trisyllabics der Gedanke, thought; der Buchſtabe, letter.

58. *D.* The Masculine Käse and the Neuter Collectives with prefix Ge⸗ and suffix ⸗e add ⸗s in the Gen. Sing. and ⸗n in the Dat. Plural:

Sing.			
	N.	der Käse	das Gemälde
	A.	den Käse	das Gemälde
	G.	des Käses	des Gemäldes
	D.	dem Käse	dem Gemälde
Plur.	N.	die Käse	die Gemälde
	A.	die Käse	die Gemälde
	G.	der Käse	der Gemälde
	D.	den Käsen	den Gemälden.

59. *E.* Neuters in ⸗mal and ⸗tum, and the two Masculines Irrtum, error, Reichtum, wealth, form the plural by modifying and adding ⸗er:

das Herzogtum, duchy, die Herzogtümer; das Denkmal, monument, die Denkmäler.

INDEX

The numbers refer to sections. Where a subject covers two or more successive sections, the number of the first section only is given.

For EU product safety concerns, contact us at Calle de José Abascal, 56–1°,
28003 Madrid, Spain or eugpsr@cambridge.org.

 www.ingramcontent.com/pod-product-compliance
Ingram Content Group UK Ltd.
Pitfield, Milton Keynes, MK11 3LW, UK
UKHW012335130625
459647UK00009B/291